The International Table Tennis Federation Handbook for Match Officials (2014)

乒乓球国际竞赛官员手册

(2014)

中国乒乓球协会　编译
Chinese Table Tennis Association

人民体育出版社
PEOPLE'S SPORTS PUBLISHING HOUSE

图书在版编目（CIP）数据

乒乓球国际竞赛官员手册. 2014 / 中国乒乓球协会编译. -- 北京 : 人民体育出版社, 2014（2024.3重印）
ISBN 978-7-5009-4737-0

Ⅰ. ①乒… Ⅱ. ①中… Ⅲ. ①乒乓球运动－竞赛规则－手册 Ⅳ. ①G846.4-62

中国版本图书馆CIP数据核字(2014)第295420号

*
人民体育出版社出版发行
三河市紫恒印装有限公司印刷
新 华 书 店 经 销
*
850×1168 32开本 7.25印张 160千字
2015年1月第1版 2024年3月第8次印刷
印数：12,001—14,000册
*
ISBN 978-7-5009-4737-0
定价：35.00元

社址：北京市东城区体育馆路8号（天坛公园东门）
电话：67151482（发行部） 邮编：100061
传真：67151483 邮购：67118491
网址：www.psphpress.com
（购买本社图书，如遇有缺损页可与邮购部联系）

前　言

中国乒乓球协会组织编译出版《乒乓球国际竞赛官员手册》（2014 版本），旨在指导我国乒乓球裁判员更好地应用国际规则和规程。为了保持世界范围内乒乓球竞赛管理的一致性，在不同的比赛或不同国家和地区比赛时，对规则的执行不存在很大的差异，国际乒联裁判长和裁判员委员会制定了一些操作程序，并提出了相应的要求。本《手册》涉及的主要是裁判员和副裁判员的职责和行为规范，也包括一部分控制比赛的职责。本《手册》也可为运动员、教练员了解和执行规则提供帮助。

中国乒乓球协会副秘书长张晓蓬，中国乒协裁判委员会主任赵霞，中国乒协裁委会副主任孙麒麟、张桦和徐昱玫、冯政、刘文珂，以及国家体育总局乒羽中心外联部部长柳屹等参加了本《手册》的撰编、翻译、审校和审核等工作，特致谢意。

中国乒乓球协会

2014 年 8 月

目 录

FOREWORD
前言

Sections of previous editions have been modified with the object of providing clearer guidance and hence more consistency in the application of laws and regulations. Comments and suggestions for additions or improvements are welcome and may be sent to the Chair of the Umpires and Referees Committee.

URC - ITTF

February 2014

对先前版本做了部分的修改，目的在于提供更具体的指导，从而更加一致地运用规则和规程。欢迎向裁判员和裁判长委员会主席提出增加或改进的意见或建议。

国际乒联–裁判员和裁判长委员会

2014 年 2 月

First edition March 1982

Second edition September 1983

Third edition January 1989

Fourth edition September 1989

Fifth edition September 1991

Sixth edition November 1993

Seventh edition September 1995

Eighth edition October 1997

Ninth edition July 2000
Tenth edition June 2004
Eleventh edition December 2005
Twelfth edition December 2006
Thirteenth edition August 2007
Fourteenth edition June 2011
Fifteenth edition February 2014
Published by
The International Table Tennis Federation
ISBN 0 946587 69 8

1982 年 3 月	第 1 版
1983 年 9 月	第 2 版
1989 年 1 月	第 3 版
1989 年 9 月	第 4 版
1991 年 9 月	第 5 版
1993 年 11 月	第 6 版
1995 年 9 月	第 7 版
1997 年 10 月	第 8 版
2000 年 7 月	第 9 版
2004 年 6 月	第 10 版
2005 年 12 月	第 11 版
2006 年 12 月	第 12 版
2007 年 8 月	第 13 版
2011 年 6 月	第 14 版
2014 年 2 月	第 15 版

由国际乒乓球联合会出版 ISBN 0 946587 69 8

The International Table Tennis Federation (ITTF), founded in 1926, is the world-governing body of the sport with 218 member Associations in the world.

The ITTF supervises the staging of annual World Championships, which involve over 800 players from all continents, and several other world title events. Its main function is to govern and develop the sport for the benefit of over thirty million competitive players in all parts of the world.

Table tennis is both an Olympic and Paralympic sport and is in the programme of the respective Summer Olympic and Paralympic Games.

国际乒乓球联合会（ITTF）成立于1926年，是乒乓球运动的全球管理机构，具有全世界218个会员协会。

国际乒联监管每年有各大洲近800名运动员参加的世界锦标赛和其他世界比赛的举办，其主要功能是为了超过3000万乒乓球运动员的利益在全球管理和发展乒乓球运动。

乒乓球是奥运会和残奥会运动并且分别是奥运会和残奥会的比赛项目。

1 INTRODUCTION

1 序言

1.1 The purpose of this booklet is to guide match officials on the application of laws and regulations, and it should be read in conjunction with the current ITTF Handbook or Rules booklet. It deals mainly with the duties of umpires and assistant umpires, but it includes also aspects of the referee's duties in relation to the control of matches. The Handbook for Tournament Referees covers the wider duties of a tournament referee.

1.1 出版这本小册子的目的是为了指导竞赛官员应用规则和规程，此书应和现行《国际乒联手册》或《规则》一起阅读。本《手册》涉及的主要是裁判员和副裁判员的职责，但也包括一部分关于裁判长控制比赛的职责。《竞赛裁判长手册》包括竞赛裁判长更多的职责。

1.2 Players are entitled to expect consistency in the conduct of matches and should not be expected to have to make continual adjustment to different procedures in different competitions or different countries. In order to encourage consistency, the ITTF Umpires and Referees Committee (URC) has produced a summary of recommended procedures for match officials and this is included as Appendix A.

1.2 参赛运动员有权希望在竞赛管理方面保持一致性，不希望在不同的比赛中或在不同国家比赛时，总是要进行调整以适应不同的比赛程序。为了保证一致性，国际乒联裁判长和裁判员委员会（URC）已经为竞赛官员制定了一个推荐程序摘要，可参见附录A。

1.3 Appendix B contains the ITTF directives for match officials at World title competitions, including World Championships and ITTF sanctioned events; these directives are not mandatory for other competitions but they are often adopted for Continental and Open International Championships.

Appendix C describes the qualification of umpires and Appendix I is a summary of law and regulation changes made since the last edition in 2007.

1.3 附录B包含国际乒联在世界级比赛（包括世界锦标赛和其他国际乒联认可的赛事）中给竞赛官员发出的指令，这些指令虽然不强制运用到其他竞赛，但在洲际锦标赛和国际公开赛中经常被采用。

附录C阐述了裁判员的资格，附录I扼要介绍了自2007版以来规则和规程的修改。

2 LAWS AND REGULATIONS

2 规则和规程

2.1 Applicability

The first requirement of a match official is a sound knowledge of the rules, comprising laws and regulations, which govern competitive table tennis, complemented by a clear understanding of the extent to which they apply to different types of competition. The relevant information is contained in Chapters 2, 3 and 4 of the ITTF Handbook.

2.1 适用性

竞赛官员的首要条件是对控制乒乓球比赛的条例，包括对规则和规程的全面掌握，再加上在不同类型比赛中对规则和规程适用范围的正确理解。相关信息包括在《国际乒联手册》的第二、三、四章中。

2.2 Laws

The "Laws of Table Tennis", referred to hereafter as "laws", are contained in Chapter 2. The laws apply to all international play and are generally adopted by Associations for their domestic competitions, although any Association has the right to introduce variations for competitions that concern only its own players. A law can be changed only at a General Meeting, with the agreement of a 75% majority of those voting.

2.2 规则

第二章“乒乓球比赛规则”（以下简称“规则”），适用于所有的国际比赛，并且被各协会普遍采用于国内比赛。虽然任何一个协会均有权在仅有自己选手参加的国内比赛中有所变化，但规则的修改只能由国际乒联代表大会做出，并且须经四分之三以上代表投票通过。

2.3 Regulations

2.3 规程

2.3.1 Chapter 3 contains the "Regulations for International Competitions", referred to hereafter as "regulations", which apply, in general, to all international competitions. The additional regulations for world title events, including World Championships, are given in Chapter 4. These regulations can be changed only at a meeting of the ITTF Board of Directors, by a simple majority of those voting.

2.3.1 第三章“国际比赛规程”（以下简称“规程”），一般来说适用于所有国际比赛。第四章给出了包括世界锦标赛之类冠名世界比赛的附加规程。国际比赛规程的修改只能由国际乒联理事会做出，并且须经简单多数投票通过。

3 TYPES OF COMPETITION

3 竞赛类型

3.1 Open Tournaments

3.1 公开赛

3.1.1 An open tournament is a competition, organized with the authority of the Association in whose territory it is held, which is open for entry to the players of any Association. In all such tournaments there may be minor variations of the regulations where the organizing authority is unable or unwilling to meet all of the requirements, usually in respect of playing conditions such as playing space.

3.1.1 公开赛是指由当地协会主办，所有协会的运动员均可报名参加的比赛。在这样的比赛中，当主办方无法或不能够满足所有必需条件（通常在比赛条件方面，比如赛区空间）时，规程可有较小的变化。

3.1.2 Where an open tournament does not comply with a particular regulation, the entry form must state clearly the nature and the extent of any variations, so that intending competitors will know in advance the limitations that will apply.

A competitor who submits such an entry form is assumed to have understood and accepted the limitations, and the tournament will then be conducted under the modified regulations.

3.1.2 公开赛如有不符合某些规程条文的地方，必须在报名表中特别说明变动的性质和程度，以便有意向参加比赛者事先了解这些变动。递交了报名表的参赛者则被认为已理解和接受了这些变动，这样公开赛就按修改后的规程进行。

3.1.3 Each season, an Association may nominate one senior, one junior and one veterans' open tournament which it organises as its Senior, Junior or Veterans' Open International Championships, and for such a tournament the regulations can be modified only with the permission of the ITTF Executive Committee. Similarly, any variations for World Championships must be authorised by the ITTF Board of Directors and for Continental Championships by the appropriate Continental Federation. An Association, in addition, may also organise a Para table tennis tournament.

3.1.3 在每一赛季，任何一个国际乒联会员协会都可以申办一次国际成年、青年或元老公开锦标赛，并且只有国际乒联执行委员会的许可，才能修改此类比赛的规程。同样地，任何对世界锦标赛规程的修改，都必须得到国际乒联理事会的批准。洲锦标赛规程的变化，必须得到相应洲联合会的批准。另外，一个协会也可以组织一次残疾人乒乓球比赛。

3.1.4 Since 1996, a number of Open International Championships have been included in a "World Tour Circuit" (previously known as Pro-Tour Circuit). They are organized di rectly under the auspices of the ITTF and, from time to time, they incorporate experimental variations of Laws and Regulations authorized by the ITTF Board of Directors. Such variations may apply to all World Tour tournaments in a season or be on an individual basis, and details will be given in the relevant entry form.

3.1.4 从 1996 年开始，一些国际公开锦标赛被纳入国际乒联举办的系列职业巡回赛中。这些比赛直接由国际乒联主办，有时会执行经国际乒联理事会授权作为实验性的规则和规程。这些变化的规则和规程会在一个赛季职业巡回赛的所有站或一站比赛中执行，变化的细节将在相关的报名表中加以说明。

3.2 Restricted Tournaments

3.2 限制赛

3.2.1 Domestic tournaments, in which all the players are from the same Association and tournaments which are restricted to players from a defined area or to members of specific groups or professions are not automatically covered by the regulations. For these competitions the organising authority has the right to decide which of the regulations will apply and what variations, if any, it wishes to make.

3.2.1 来自同一协会的运动员参加的国内比赛以及参赛运动员仅限于某个地区，或者仅限于某些组织或职业的比赛，不受国际乒联规程限制，组织机构有权决定采用哪个规程或做出某种变化。

3.3 Other International Competitions

3.3 其他国际比赛

3.3.1 International team matches, other than those in

World or Continental Championships, normally observe all the regulations, but the participating Associations may agree on modifications. In these and other international competitions, it should be assumed that all the appropriate regulations are in force unless the published conditions of the event state that there are exceptions and make clear what the exceptions are.

3.3.1 除了世界锦标赛和洲际锦标赛，国际团体比赛通常应遵循所有国际比赛规程，但参赛协会可以协商修改规程。除非事先说明并详细阐明有变动事项，否则国际比赛规程应被认为适用于此类和其他各类国际比赛。

4 MATCH OFFICIALS

4 竞赛官员

4.1 Referee

4.1 裁判长

4.1.1 For every competition as a whole a referee is appointed, usually with one or more deputies who can act on his or her behalf. The referee or an authorised deputy must be present in the playing hall throughout play, to decide any question of rule interpretation, on which he or she is the sole authority, and generally to ensure that the competition is conducted in accordance with the relevant laws and regulations.

4.1.1 每个比赛必须指派 1 名裁判长，通常同时指派 1 名或几名副裁判长，以便在裁判长缺席时代理其职权。裁判长或授权的副裁判长必须自始至终亲临赛场，对任何有关规则解释的问题做出决定，而且他（她）是此类问题的唯一权威，以保证比赛在相关的规则和规程下进行。

4.1.2 Where the referee is the sole arbiter, such as in allowing a temporary suspension of play for injury or disqualifying a player for misbehaviour, he or she must act consistently and avoid any suspicion of partiality to particular players. In major competitions it is recommended that the referee and his or her deputies be from different Associations, so that there is always a “neutral” official to adjudicate in a dispute.

4.1.2 对诸如因伤要求暂停比赛或取消不良行为运动员比赛资格等事例，裁判长是唯一的裁决者。他（她）必须保持公正，避免任何偏袒特殊运动员的嫌疑。在重要的比赛中，建议裁判长和副裁判长来自不同的协会，以便在裁定争议时始终保持“中立”。

4.1.3 The referee is responsible for the appointment of match officials. Although he or she will not normally make such appointments himself or herself he or she must be satisfied that the officials are competent and that they act fairly and consistently. He or she should explain to the umpires, in his or her pre-tournament briefing, how he or she expects laws and regulations to be applied, especially where any of these are new or might be contentious.

4.1.3 裁判长的职责包括指派其他竞赛官员，虽然他（她）通常不会亲自指派，但他（她）必须确信被指派的比赛官员是能够胜任的，并且能公正、一致地执行规则和规程。裁判长在赛前短会中，应向裁判员解释他（她）期望执行规则和规程的尺度，尤其是对那些新的或可能会有争议的规则和规程。

4.1.4 The players are under the jurisdiction of the referee from the time at which they arrive at the playing venue until the time at which they leave it. The practice hall or area is considered to be part of the playing venue.

4.1.4 运动员从到达比赛场地的那一刻直至离开，必须在裁判长的管辖之下，练习场地也被认为是比赛场地的一部分。

4.2 Umpire

4.2 裁判员

4.2.1 For each match there is an umpire, whose primary duty is to decide the result of each rally. In principle, the umpire has no discretionary powers, but he or she is required to exercise judgment in applying some laws and regulations, such as deciding whether a rally should be a let because a player's service or return may have been affected by circumstances outside the player's control, or whether a player's behavior is acceptable.

4.2.1 每场比赛必须指派 1 名裁判员，其基本职责是根据事实决定每个回合的结果。原则上，裁判员无自由裁决的权利，但某些规则和规程的执行却要求他（她）行使裁决权，例如：当运动员的发球或还击由于无法控制的环境干扰而受到影响时，决定该回合是否为重发球，或决定运动员的行为是否可以接受。

4.2.2 Where the umpire is officiating alone, his or she has the final decision on all questions of fact that arise during a match, including decisions on all edge balls and on all aspects of service. In these circumstances he or she is directly responsible also for timing the duration of play, but when the expedite system is in operation he or she is assisted by another official who acts as stroke counter.

4.2.2 当一名裁判员单独执法时，他（她）对一场比赛中发生的所有问题做出最终的决定，包括擦边球和所有有关发球方面的判定。在这种情况下，他（她）也直接负责比赛时间的掌控。但当实行轮换发球法时，需要有另一名裁判员来协助他（她）计数。

4.2.3 Although the umpire is obliged to accept certain decisions made by other match officials he or she is entitled to seek an explanation if he or she believes that an official has made a decision that is outside his or her jurisdiction. If, on enquiry, he or she finds that an official has acted in this way he or she can overrule the decision wrongly made by that official, either by reversing it or, more usually, by declaring the rally a let.

4.2.3 有时裁判员必须接受由其他竞赛官员做出的某些裁决，但如果他（她）认为该官员所做的裁决超越了其权限，有权要求解释。经询问，如果该官员确实超越了权限，他（她）可以否决其所做的错误裁决，或者纠正，或者（更常见的）宣判该回合为重发球。

4.2.4 The umpire should be about 2 - 3 meters from the side of the table, in line with the net, preferably on a slightly raised chair, although this is not essential for singles. For doubles, the umpire is advised to stand if his or her seat is not high enough for him or her to see clearly whether in service the ball bounces on the correct half-courts. Standing for singles is not recommended, because it unnecessarily obstructs the view of spectators.

4.2.4 裁判员应该坐在球台一侧2~3米处，与球网成一直线。裁判椅应该稍高一些，虽然单打比赛时这不是基本的要求。双打比赛中，如果裁判椅不够高，以致裁判员看不清发球是否落在正确的台区时，裁判员应该站立执法。单打比赛中，裁判员不应站立，以免挡住观众的视线。

4.2.5 The players are under the jurisdiction of the umpire from the time at which they arrive at the playing area until the time at which they leave it.

4.2.5 运动员从到达比赛区域的那一刻直至离开，应处于裁判员的管辖之下。

4.3 Assistant Umpire

4.3 副裁判员

4.3.1 For international competitions an assistant umpire is appointed and he or she takes over or shares some of the umpire's duties. For example, an assistant umpire is solely responsible for decisions on edge balls at the side of the table nearest to him or her, and he or she has the same power as the umpire to decide the legality of a players' service action, whether a player obstructs the ball and some of the conditions for a let.

4.3.1 国际比赛必须指派1名副裁判员，由他（她）接管或分担裁判员的某些职责。例如：副裁判员全权决定靠近他（她）一侧球台的擦边球，同样有权决定运动员发球的合法性、运动员阻挡和某些情况的重发球。

4.3.2 If either the umpire or the assistant umpire decides that a player's service action is illegal, that a player obstructs the ball, that the ball in service touches the net or that the conditions of play are disturbed in a way which could affect the outcome of the rally, that decision stands.

4.3.2 无论是裁判员还是副裁判员，均有权判定发球员的发球不合法、运动员阻挡、发球擦网或者比赛条件受到干扰可能会影响该回合结果，且该判定有效。

4.3.3 Nevertheless, a decision taken by one of these officials may in some circumstances be pre-empted by a decision of the other. For instance, whether or not the ball touches the edge of the playing surface on the side nearest to the assistant umpire may be irrelevant if the umpire has already seen a player move the playing surface. Similarly, a service that is judged illegal by the assistant umpire may not be penalized if the umpire has previously decided that the rally is a let because a ball from another table has come into the playing area.

4.3.3 然而，在某种情况下，他们当中一个人的判定可能会被另一个人的先行判定所取代。例如：假如裁判员已经看到运动员的不执拍手触及了比赛台面，他（她）就可能不予注意球是否在靠近副裁判员一侧擦边了；同样，如果裁判员因为外界球的进入而先判定该回合为重发球，则副裁判员判定的发球违例就不再失分了。

4.3.4 The assistant umpire should be seated directly opposite the umpire, in line with the net, and at about the same distance from the table. The assistant umpire should not stand for doubles.

4.3.4 副裁判员应坐在裁判员的对面，与球网成一直线，距球台的距离与裁判员相同。双打比赛时，副裁判员不要站立。

4.4 Timekeeper

4.4 计时员

4.4.1 An assistant umpire may act as timekeeper, but some umpires prefer to carry out this function themselves, perhaps because they wish to decide for themselves how much time to allow for interruptions in play. The timekeeper is required to monitor the duration of practice, of play in a game, of intervals between games and of any authorized suspension of play, and his or her decision is final on the time that has elapsed.

4.4.1 计时员可由副裁判员担任，但有些裁判员更愿意自己负责，或许他们希望自己掌握比赛中断时间的长短。计时员必须控制赛前练习、一局比赛、局与局之间的间歇及任何经批准的中断时间。计时员在有关时间的问题上有最终决定权。

4.5 Stroke Counter

4.5 计数员

4.5.1 Stroke counting when the expedite system is in operation is normally undertaken by a separate official, but the assistant umpire also can act as stroke counter. The stroke counter's duty is solely to count the return strokes of the receiver and his or her decision on this question of fact cannot be overruled. If the assistant umpire does act as stroke counter he or she still retains his or her full responsibilities as assistant umpire.

4.5.1 执行轮换发球法时的计数，通常由另外的官员担任，但副裁判员也可担任。计数员的职责只是计接发球方的还击数，其他人不得更改他（她）对这个事实做出的判定。如果副裁判员没有担任计数员，他（她）继续执行副裁判员的全部职责。

4.6 Appeals

4.6 申诉

4.6.1 A player, or in a team match his or her captain, may appeal against what he or she believes to be a wrong rule interpretation by the umpire, assistant umpire or stroke counter, but no appeal may be made against a decision on fact by any of these officials in accordance with his or her designated authority. Such an appeal may be made to the referee, whose decision is final on any question of rule interpretation.

4.6.1 运动员或团体比赛中的队长，如果认为裁判员、副裁判员或计数员对规则的解释是错误的，可以提出申诉，但不得对他们中任何一个人在其职权范围内就事实所做的判定提出申诉。此类申诉应向裁判长提出，裁判长对任何解释规则问题的决定为最终决定。

4.6.2 If, however, the player or captain believes that the referee is incorrect a further appeal may be made, by the player's Association, to the ITTF Rules Committee. This committee will give a ruling for future occasions but it cannot change the decision already made by the referee. An appeal may be made also to the tournament management committee against a referee's decision on any matter not covered by rule.

4.6.2　不过，如果运动员或队长认为裁判长裁决错误，可以通过其协会向国际乒联规则委员会进一步提出申诉。规则委员会将做出裁定，作为今后的准则，但不能改变裁判长已做出的裁决。就裁判长对未包括在规则中的任何问题所做的决定也可以向竞赛管理委员会提出申诉。

4.6.3　In responding to appeals, the referee must take care to observe the relevant procedures. In an individual event, he or she should deal only with the player or pair; a team captain or coach should not be allowed to intercede on his or her player's behalf, but an interpreter may assist where there is a language difficulty. In a team match, any protest by a player that is not supported by his or her team captain should be ignored.

4.6.3　对待申诉，裁判长必须注意按相应的程序来处理。单项比赛中，他（她）应该只接受运动员本人或配对运动员的申诉，不允许队长或教练员代表其运动员提出请求；如存在语言障碍则允许有翻译帮助。团体比赛中，一名运动员的任何抗议未得到其队长的支持将不予理睬。

4.6.4　When the appeal is against the action of a match official, only that official should participate in the argument of the case. The referee may at some stage wish to hear the evidence or opinion of another official or a witness, but once that person has made his or her statement he or she should take no further part in any discussion, and interference by anyone not directly concerned must be firmly discouraged.

4.6.4　当出现对某竞赛官员提出申诉时，只有该竞赛官员可加入辩论。有时，裁判长可能会征询同场地其他竞赛官员或证人的证词或意见，但其陈述完毕就不得继续参加讨论，任何无关人员不得介入。

4.7 Replacement

4.7 更换裁判员

4.7.1 There may be occasions during a competition, either before a match or after play has started, when there is a question about the ability of a match official to carry out the duties for which he or she has been appointed. Such occasions are rare but when they do occur the referee must be ready to use his or her authority to deal with the matter, possibly replacing the official concerned if that is the only appropriate course of action.

4.7.1 比赛期间，不管是一场比赛开始前还是已经开始，有时会出现临场裁判员是否有能力履行其职责的问题。虽然这种情况很少发生，但一旦发生，裁判长就必须行使权力来处理。如果更换裁判员是唯一合适的方式就应进行更换。

4.7.2 The essential question for the referee is whether the appointment of a particular official, or the retention of an official already appointed, is likely to lead to an unfair result in the match. If an official is acting correctly and consistently and is not showing deliberate partiality it would be unreasonable for the referee to replace him or her simply because his or her decisions might affect one player or pair more than the other.

4.7.2 裁判长必须考虑的是：更换与不更换裁判员，哪个可能导致比赛结果不公平。假如一名裁判员的执法是正确的、一致的，没有蓄意偏袒的迹象，那么仅仅因为他（她）的判定可能对一方的影响比另一方大就将其更换掉，这是不合理的。

4.7.3 A complaint by a player that an umpire is too strict in his or her application of the laws or that he or she has been the subject of a previous protest by the player does not automatically disqualify him or her from officiating at a match in which that player is due to take part. Similarly, disputes between a match official and a player or captain during a match, however protracted, do not necessarily justify the replacement of that official.

4.7.3 裁判员被一名运动员抱怨执法太严厉或者曾是运动员抗议的对象，不应成为取消该裁判员执法那位运动员要参加的比赛的理由。同样地，比赛中，裁判员与运动员或队长之间持续地争执未必就成为更换该裁判员的依据。

4.7.4 Occasional mistakes by an umpire, especially if quickly corrected, would not normally justify his or her removal and it is generally better for the referee not to intervene during a game even when mistakes are more persistent, provided it is clear that the outcome of the match is not being prejudiced. Account must be taken, however, particularly in staged matches, of the possible effect on public presentation.

4.7.4 一个裁判员偶尔出错，尤其是能很快纠正，则不足以成为更换的理由；即使错误一再出现，但比赛结果明显不会受到影响，裁判长通常最好不去干预该局比赛。然而，必须考虑到观众可能的反响，特别是重要场次的比赛。

4.7.5 If, and only if, the referee is satisfied that the retention of an official is likely to prejudice a fair result, owing to complete loss of confidence by the players in the official's competence or judgment, that official may be replaced by another. The change should be made with the least possible fuss and the referee should explain carefully to the replaced official the reason for his or her action, avoiding any public display of criticism.

4.7.5 且只有当运动员对裁判员的能力或执法完全失去信任，裁判长确信继续留用该裁判员可能影响比赛的公正结果，裁判长才可更换裁判员。更换时，要尽量减小影响，同时，应向被更换的裁判员谨慎地解释原因，避免在公众面前显出批评。

4.7.6 Where an official is replaced for making wrong decisions, the score resulting from these decisions cannot be changed if they were made on questions of fact within his or her jurisdiction. If they were made through a misinterpretation of rule or were outside his or her jurisdiction, consideration may be given to replaying any game whose result was affected, but it is generally better to proceed from the score that has been reached.

4.7.6 当一个裁判员因为裁决错误而被更换时，在他（她）权限内根据事实所做的判决不得更改。假如错误的产生明显是由于错误理解了规则或者超出了权限，那么可以考虑将比分受到影响的比赛重新开始。不过，通常最好还是从已有的比分开始继续比赛。

4.8 Presentation (See also Appendices A, D, E, F & G)

4.8 精神面貌（参见附录 A、D、E、F 和 G）

4.8.1 In addition to their responsibility for ensuring a fair result, match officials have an essential part to play in the presentation of a match. This should not, however, encourage them to indulge in personal showmanship and the best tribute to a good team of match officials is that they are not noticed, because they control play so unobtrusively that players and spectators can concentrate totally on the match.

4.8.1 裁判员除了基本的职责——保证比赛公平竞争外，还在赛场的面貌方面起着必不可少的作用。然而，这并不是鼓励他们去沉湎于个人表演。一支好的裁判员队伍是不引人注目的，由于他们不引人注意地控制着比赛，因此运动员和观众才能全神贯注于比赛的进程。

4.8.2 While on duty match officials should look alert and interested in the match at which they are officiating. Players, to whom each match is a serious matter, do not always welcome a jocular or light-hearted attitude. Officials should not leave their places during a match unless they need to do so for a specific purpose, such as to retrieve the match ball at the end of a game or to restore the position of surrounds.

4.8.2 执行任务时，裁判员应该保持机敏并将注意力集中于自己正在执裁的比赛上。对于运动员来说比赛是件严肃的事，他们不欢迎裁判员的诙谐和轻松态度。在比赛过程中，裁判员不应离开自己的座位，除非为了某种特殊目的，诸如在一局比赛结束后收回比赛用球或将挡板摆放整齐。

4.8.3 Even when off-duty, match officials should take care not to behave in a way which may prejudice their authority or which may reflect unfavorably on their Associations or on the sport. Good relationships with players are important, but care should be taken not to appear unduly friendly with particular players or to give any indication of partiality. Public criticism of other officials or organizers should be avoided.

4.8.3 即使不执行任务，裁判员也应该注意不要让不庄重的行为损害自己的权威或损坏本协会或乒乓球运动的声誉。与运动员保持良好的关系是很重要的，但要注意避免与某些运动员的关系过于友好或有偏向的嫌疑。要避免公开批评其他官员或主办者。

4.8.4 Match officials are also responsible for the appearance of the playing area during a match. It should be kept tidy and free from unnecessary people and equipment, and any disturbance of the table or surrounds should be corrected immediately. Only officials directly concerned with a match should be allowed in the play area, positioned so that they are as unobtrusive as possible consistent with their being able to carry out their duties.

4.8.4 在比赛期间，裁判员也有责任保持比赛赛场的外貌。保持比赛场地的整齐、干净，清除无关人员、设备，球台与挡板被弄乱应立即复位。只有与本场有关的裁判员可以进入比赛区域，裁判员的位置在能够执行任务的情况下，尽可能地保持不引人注目。

4.8.5 Organizers, normally in conjunction with the referee, usually set a limit for the number of persons allowed on the “team bench” and, in an individual event, there may also be a limit on the number of people allowed to accompany the players or pairs. It is the duty of the umpire to ensure that any such limits are observed and, if necessary, play should be suspended until those not entitled to be there have withdrawn.

4.8.5 主办方通常和裁判长一起，会对团体赛中教练员座席人数有所限制，单项比赛对允许陪同运动员（进入比赛区域）的人数也有规定。裁判员有责任确保这些规定被遵守，必要时裁判员应暂停比赛，将无资格的人请出教练席。

4.8.6 It is advisable to close jackets when entering the field of play, and during the pre- or post-match presentation. However, whilst sitting down, it may be better to open the jacket for easier arm movements. It is important, at all tournaments, to make professional presentation a habit and something that the umpire feels natural and comfortable with at all times. (See Appendix F)

4.8.6 当进入比赛区域做赛前或赛后介绍时，可将上衣的纽扣系好；而当坐下时，解开上衣的纽扣以便手臂运动。在任何比赛的任何时候，裁判员均应对职业表现养成习惯并应感到自然、舒适，这一点很重要（参见附录 F）。

4.9 Uniform for Umpires

4.9 裁判员服装

4.9.1 Most Associations have adopted standards of clothing for their match officials, consisting usually of a jacket and trousers or skirt of specified colors, but the same clothing may not be suitable in all environments. For instance, in very warm conditions it may be intolerable for an official to have to wear a jacket throughout what may prove to be a long match, while some playing halls may be uncomfortably cold.

4.9.1　大多数协会已采纳了裁判服的标准。通常包括规定颜色的一件上衣和一条裤子或裙子，但同样的衣服并不适合在所有环境下穿着。比如，在非常闷热的环境中，裁判员穿着裁判服执裁了一场时间很长的比赛，可能汗湿衣衫。而有些赛场大厅，穿着同样的服装则可能冷得够呛。

4.9.2　In these circumstances the team of officials for a match should agree among themselves reasonable variations so that if, for example, they need to wear pullovers, these are all of the same color. The most important consideration is that the officials are neatly dressed, as uniformly as is practicable, but it should be confirmed that any proposed changes to the normal uniform are acceptable to the organizers of the competition.

4.9.2　在这种情况下，一次比赛的所有裁判员可共同协商确定如何对着装进行改变，如都穿颜色相同的套衫。最重要的是裁判员的服装必须整洁，尽可能穿着一致。必须强调的是，改变裁判服应得到比赛主办方的许可。

4.9.3　The URC has adopted a standard umpire's uniform for World Title Events (Appendix G). For other ITTF sanctioned events, International Umpires may wear the uniform of their Associations or the ITTF IU Uniform.

4.9.3　对冠名的世界比赛，裁判长和裁判员委员会已经采用了标准的裁判员服装（附录 G）。国际乒联许可的其他比赛，裁判员可以穿着所属协会的服装或国际乒联国际级裁判员的服装。

4.9.4　Unless approved by the referee for religious or medical reasons, hats or headgear should not be worn. Tracksuits, windbreakers, etc. should never be worn.

4.9.4 除非因为宗教或健康的原因并得到裁判长的同意，否则不允许佩戴帽子或头饰。长袖运动服、风衣等绝对不允许穿着。

4.9.5 In some events, such as the Olympic and Paralympic Games, the organisers provide a uniform for match officials which should be worn during the event.

4.9.5 在某些比赛，如奥运会和残奥会中，主办方为比赛官员提供赛时穿着的制服。

5 LAYING CONDITIONS

5 比赛条件

5.1 The referee has the final decision on the acceptability of playing conditions but it is usually the umpire who is first aware of possible deficiencies, especially those that arise once an event has started. The umpire must, therefore, know the requirements of the relevant laws and regulations so that he or she can report promptly to the referee any variation that is not within his or her power to correct.

5.1 比赛条件的可接受性由裁判长最后裁定。但通常是裁判员首先意识到可能存在的缺陷，尤其是那些开赛后才出现的缺陷。因此，裁判员必须熟悉有关规则、规程的规定，以便能及时向裁判长报告他（她）无权纠正的缺陷。

5.2 The playing space and the level of lighting will normally have been checked when the playing hall is set up and the tables and nets will have been properly installed. The umpire should, however, satisfy himself or herself before play begins that nothing has happened to disturb the conditions of play, such as failure of a light source, displacement of a table or the surrounds or loss of tension in the net assembly.

5.2 通常在确定比赛场地时就对比赛空间及照明度进行过检查，球台、球网也已安装妥当。但裁判员还是应该在赛前亲自检查一下有无影响比赛条件的情况，诸如电源没接通、球台或挡板位置不当、球网没拉紧等。

5.3 Whenever possible, the umpire should try to correct any deficiency himself or herself but if he or she cannot do so without holding up play he or she should report promptly to the referee. The referee may defer the match until the proper playing conditions have been restored or may transfer the match to another table but, if the shortcomings are only slight, he or she and the players may agree to ignore it and play the match in less than ideal conditions.

5.3 出现缺陷，裁判员应自己设法解决，如果不停止比赛就不能解决问题，则应及时报告裁判长。裁判长可以中断比赛直到恢复适合比赛条件，或将比赛更换到另一张球台上进行。如果缺陷比较轻微，裁判长、双方运动员都同意忽略，比赛可以在不太理想的条件下继续进行。

5.4 Match officials have a responsibility to see that the advertising regulations are observed. The number, size and colouring of advertisements on equipment and fittings in and around the playing area should be checked by the referee, in time for any necessary corrections to be made before play starts. During the competition, umpires should ensure compliance with the restrictions on advertisements on players' clothing and numbers.

5.4 竞赛官员有责任检查、监督有关广告规定的执行。裁判长应检查赛场内、赛场周围器材和装置上广告的数量、颜色和尺寸，以便在比赛开始前及时进行必要的纠正。比赛期间，裁判员必须保证运动员服装和号码布上的广告符合规定。

5.5 It is important for the umpire or assistant umpire to check both the height of the net and the tension of the net-cord. This should be done prior to every match, including team matches within a team competition. It is not really satisfactory just to estimate the tension by touch and several manufacturers have produced weighted net gauges, which ensure consistency. These gauges, which weigh exactly 100g, have two steps, one at 15.25cm and the other 1cm lower. However the weighted gauge should only be used to check the tension - it is not advisable to use it for checking the height. After the height has been checked using a plastic net gauge at each end the lower step of the weighted gauge is rested on the top of the net, in the centre, and the tension adjusted until the bottom of the gauge just touches the playing surface. If necessary, quickly re-check the height at each end after the tension has been adjusted. Do not use the plastic gauge and weighted gauge at the same time. Also when checking the net it is important to ensure that the clamp is attached as close as possible to the table. Ensure that there is no cord hanging down from the net post which could affect the ball or distract the players.

5.5 检查球网的高度和张力对裁判员或副裁判员来说是一件很重要的事。每一场比赛前，包括团体比赛中的每一场，应做好球网的检查。仅靠触摸来估计网的张力是不能真正令人满意的。有一些制造商生产出了金属量网尺，确保了一致性。这种量网尺正好 100 克重，有两条边，一条边长 15.25 厘米，另一条边低 1 厘米。然而金属量网尺只能用来检查网张力而不能检查网高。当用塑料量网尺检查球网两端的高度后，将金属量网尺低的一边挂在球网中央顶部，当尺子的底部刚好触及比赛台面时，网张力就调整好了。球网张力调整过后，如有必要，快速地再次测量一下球网两端的高度。不能同时使用塑料量网尺和金属量网尺。当检查球网时，重要的是确保夹钳尽可能地贴近球台。确保悬网绳不要从网柱上垂落下来，以免影响球或分散运动员的注意力。

6 THE BALL

6 球

6.1 Type

6.1 类型

6.1.1 It is the umpire's duty to ensure that the ball used for each match is of the brand and colour specified for the competition and it is not permissible for a ball of a different kind to be used, even if both players or pairs prefer it. Any attempt by a player to substitute an alternative ball for the one supplied may be regarded as unfair behavior, to be dealt with under the appropriate regulations.

6.1.1 裁判员有责任保证每场比赛用球的品牌、颜色是比赛指定的，即使双方运动员都更喜欢使用其他型号的球也不允许。运动员任何企图用其他球替代指定用球的行为，可被认为是不良行为并按相关规程进行处理。

6.2 Choice

6.2 选择球

6.2.1 Players are not allowed to select balls in the playing area but, wherever possible, they should be given the opportu nity to do so before they come to the match table. For the match they must accept a ball taken at random by the umpire either from among those they have chosen or, if for any reason they have not chosen any, from a box of balls of the brand and colour specified for the competition.

6.2.1 不允许运动员在比赛区域内挑球，但在进入赛场前，运动员应有机会挑选比赛用球。运动员必须接受裁判员从赛前挑选的球中随机取一个球进行比赛，或者不管是何原因，如果赛前没有挑球，则由裁判员从一盒大会指定品牌和颜色的比赛用球中任意取一个进行比赛。

6.2.2 The same procedure is followed if a ball is damaged or lost during a match and has to be replaced. If this happens, the players may be allowed a short period of practice with the new ball but it must be made clear to them that this is simply to enable them to get used to its characteristics and that there is no question of their being allowed to test it and possibly ask for an alternative.

6.2.2 如果比赛期间因球破裂或打飞了而必须换球时，应按如下程序处理：运动员可用新球练习少数几个来回，但必须让他们清楚，这只是让他们熟识新球的性能，不可能允许他们检测这个球，而允许要求另换一个。

7 THE RACKET

7 球拍

7.1 Coverings

7.1 覆盖物

7.1.1 A striking surface of the racket must be covered with one of the specified materials and, whether covered or not, one side must be red and the other black. The covering should extend to the limits of, but not beyond, the blade, but some tolerance may be allowed. The referee must decide what is acceptable and advise his or her umpires accordingly but, as a guide, ±2mm would be an acceptable margin to most referees. This may particularly be the case with Para class 1 and 2 players as they often use their racket hand to push themselves back up into a sitting position after striking the ball, and, in doing so, touch the table top with their rackets. Thus an overhang can help to protect the table top and a slightly larger margin may be allowed.

7.1.1 球拍的击球面必须覆盖指定的材料，无论是否有覆盖物，球拍两面的颜色都必须一面是鲜红色，一面是黑色。覆盖物必须覆盖底板的击球部分，不得超出但可允许有一定的宽限。宽限的范围必须由裁判长决定，并要求裁判员按照他（她）所决定的宽限来执行。作为参考，大多数裁判长允许的宽限是超出或缩进 2 毫米。残障 1 级和 2 级的运动员更是如此，他们在击球后通常会借用执拍手，以球拍接触球台表面的方式将自己的身体推回到坐姿。因此，覆盖物超出可以帮助保护球台表面，一个稍大的边缘是可以允许的。

7.1.2 In competitions played under international regulations the covering must be of a type authorized by the ITTF. Coverings authorized in this way carry the ITTF logo and the maker's logo or trademark, and players are required to attach the rubber to the blade so that these identifying features are clearly visible near the handle of the striking surface so that they can be checked by the umpire.

7.1.2 在按国际竞赛规程组织的比赛中，球拍的覆盖物必须是国际乒联批准的型号，须附有国际乒联的标志和制造商的标志或商标，且运动员粘贴胶皮时必须使这些标志在击球拍面的近拍柄处清晰可见，以便裁判员检查。

7.1.3 The umpire must check the racket covering against a list of currently approved racket coverings. The presence of the ITTF marking is required but is not proof that the covering is currently authorised. The ITTF web site www.ittf.com has a list of currently approved racket coverings (LARC).

7.1.3 裁判员必须对照最新的覆盖物批准表检查球拍覆盖物。覆盖物上虽然有 ITTF 标记，但并不能证明它是国际乒联新近批准的覆盖物。国际乒联网站(www.ittf.com)有新近批准的覆盖物一览表。

7.1.4 Although only materials that comply with current laws and regulations are authorized, it cannot be assumed that a covering marked as authorized will automatically be legal.

The original sponge layer may have been replaced by one of greater thickness and gluing can cause the layer to swell, so the thickness of the covering should always be checked. The covering must be used as it has been authorised by ITTF and is not allowed to be treated in any way, either by physical, chemical or other treatment which could modify the playing properties, such as friction, colour, surface, etc, and shall successfully pass all parameters of the racket control tests.

7.1.4 虽然只有符合现行规则和规程的材料才能被许可，但并不能就此断定有许可标志的覆盖物就是合法的。因为原来的海绵层可能被替换成更厚的，胶水也可使海绵层膨胀，因此需要经常测量覆盖物的厚度。覆盖物必须是国际乒联许可的，不得经过任何物理或化学处理以改变球拍的性能，如摩擦力、颜色、外观等，并能顺利通过球拍检测的各项指标。

7.1.5 One of the most difficult decisions for an umpire or referee to make is the glossiness allowable for racket coverings. Although this can be measured with an EEL glossometer, such equipment is not usually available at a competition and some more practical means must be found. As a guide, a racket covering can be considered too glossy if letters can be clearly distinguished when, say, a net measure is placed at an angle to the racket surface. However, the umpire will only be required to check the glossiness if he or she receives a complaint from the opposing player.

7.1.5 对于裁判员和裁判长来说，判断覆盖物的光泽度是否可接受是最困难的事之一。虽然可以使用 EEL 光泽度测量仪，但这种设备在比赛中通常不一定有，因此必须找到更适用的方法。作为指导，可以用量网尺以一定角度放在球拍的表面，如果字母可以清楚地分辨出来，则可认为球拍覆盖物亮度超标。不过，裁判员只有在对方选手有抱怨时才必须检测光泽度。

7.2 Adhesives

7.2 黏合剂

7.2.1 Covering may be attached to racket blades only by means of pressure-sensitive adhesive sheets or liquid adhesives that do not contain harmful solvents. Organisers are required to provide a properly ventilated gluing area and players must not use liquid glues or the associated solvents anywhere else in the playing hall, including changing rooms and practice and spectator areas.

7.2.1 覆盖物可用压力感应胶纸或不含有毒溶剂的液体黏合剂粘贴在底板上。主办方应提供通风的粘贴区域，严禁运动员在比赛大厅包括更衣室、练习区域和观众席使用液体胶水或相关溶剂。

7.2.2 Glues containing harmful volatile compounds are no longer approved by the ITTF. ITTF has informed all players to cease using glues containing volatile compounds and any player using such glues will be doing so at his or her own risk. ITTF has implemented a zero tolerance racket testing program and protocol, using mini RAE instruments, to ensure that all rackets used by players are free of volatile compounds. Adhesives containing volatile organic solvents cannot be used at the playing venue.

7.2.2 含有有毒挥发化合物的胶水不再被国际乒联允许

使用。国际乒联已经告知运动员停止使用含有有毒挥发化合物的胶水，任何运动员使用此类胶水，风险自负。国际乒联实施了零容忍的球拍检测程序和计划，使用 mini RAE 仪器，确保所有运动员使用的球拍不含挥发性化合物。含有挥发性有机溶剂的黏合剂不得在比赛场馆使用。

7.2.3 In major competitions a racket control centre is established and rackets are tested for the presence of banned solvents, thickness, flatness, etc, normally before the matches.

7.2.3 在重要比赛中会建立一个球拍检测中心，通常在赛前检测球拍是否含有禁用溶剂、厚度、平整度等。

7.2.4 A racket that does not pass a pre-match test, will be confiscated and the player will have to use a different racket; if there is no time to test the replacement before the match, it will be tested afterwards. A racket that is found satisfactory will be marked and given to the umpire in a paper envelope (or bag if envelope is not available) for issue at the match table.

7.2.4 未通过赛前检测的球拍将会被没收，运动员将不得不使用另一块球拍；如果赛前没有时间检测更换的球拍，将在赛后检测。合格的球拍将会被做上标记并放入纸质信封（注：如果没有纸质信封可用纸袋）交给该场比赛的裁判员放在比赛球台上。

7.2.5 If a racket fails a post-match test, the offending player will be liable to penalties as detailed in Referee Directives regarding Racket Control which are available on the ITTF website.

7.2.5 若球拍未通过赛后检测，运动员可能会受到国际乒联网站裁判长指南中详尽的有关球拍检测处罚。

7.2.6 All players are entitled to have their rackets tested voluntarily without any penalties before the match. Full details of racket control can be found on the URC page of the ITTF web site.

7.2.6 所有运动员都有权在赛前将球拍送去做自愿检测，自愿检测不会招致任何处罚。球拍检测的详细信息可在国际乒联网站“裁判员和裁判长委员会”主页上找到。

7.3 Inspection

7.3 检查

7.3.1 The umpire should inspect the rackets that players intend to use, if possible before arriving at the court, but before they start their pre-match practice, so as to avoid unnecessary delay at the start of the match. This, and any subsequent inspection necessary because a damaged racket has to be replaced, should be done with as little fuss as possible. Opponents must always be given the opportunity to examine any racket that is to be used.

7.3.1 如有可能，裁判员应在运动员到达球台之前，而不是在开始赛前练习之前对其将要使用的球拍进行检查，从而避免对比赛的延误。此类检查以及随后因为更换损坏的球拍而必须进行的检查，应尽可能地使影响面小些。但是，任何情况下都必须给对手以合适的机会检查将要使用的球拍。

7.3.2 If the umpire considers that a racket is illegal he or she should explain why to the player. Even where this is a question of fact, such as an over-thick covering, the player may not accept the ruling. In such a situation the matter must be reported to the referee, whose decision will be final. Similarly, if an opponent objects to a racket, which the umpire considers acceptable, the referee must decide whether the objection is justified.

7.3.2 假如裁判员认为球拍不合法，他（她）应该向该运动员清楚地解释原因。即使是像覆盖物厚度超过标准之类的事实，运动员也可能不接受裁决。遇这种情形必须报告裁判长，裁判长拥有最后的裁决权。同样地，假如对手反对而裁判员认为可用，也必须报告裁判长，由裁判长做出裁决。

7.3.3 A player is not allowed to change a racket during a match unless it is accidentally damaged so badly that it cannot be used. If it is discovered that a player has changed an undamaged racket the umpire should immediately suspend play and report to the referee, who may disqualify the player.

7.3.3 比赛中，不允许运动员更换球拍，除非球拍意外损坏不能使用。如果发现运动员未经允许更换未损坏的球拍，裁判员必须立刻中断比赛，报告裁判长。裁判长可取消该运动员的比赛资格。

7.3.4 Players must normally leave their rackets on the table during the intervals between games and must not remove them without the specific agreement of the umpire. If, with the agreement of the umpire, a player removes his or her racket during an interval for any reason, the umpire and the opponent must be given the opportunity to inspect the racket, or its replacement, before the next game starts. The only exception to this is a disabled player whose racket is strapped to his or her hand.

7.3.4 在局与局的比赛间歇，运动员必须将球拍留在球台上，未经裁判员的特别批准，不得拿走球拍。无论何种原因，如果运动员在局与局的比赛间歇，经裁判员同意拿走球拍，或更换球拍，均必须在下局比赛开始前，允许裁判员和对手有合适的机会来检查球拍。唯一的例外就是将球拍绑在手上的残疾人运动员。

7.4 Damage

7.4 损坏

7.4.1 A racket which is legal when a player starts to use it may become damaged to an extent which invalidates its legality by, perhaps, destroying the continuity of the covering or the uniformity of pimples over a significant part of the surface. If a player wishes to continue with a damaged racket and the umpire has any doubt about its continuing legality he or she should immediately report to the referee.

7.4.1 比赛开始时符合规则规定的球拍，在比赛中可能被损坏，并可能严重损坏到不符合规则，例如覆盖物的整体性或大部分胶皮颗粒的均匀性损坏。如果运动员要求继续使用已损坏的球拍，而裁判员怀疑其继续使用是否合法时，应立即报告裁判长。

7.4.2 In deciding whether to allow further use of a damaged racket the referee should consider primarily the interests of the opponent. The ball is likely to rebound unpredictably from a damaged surface and this could cause difficulties for both players, although the player who wishes to use the racket has implicitly accepted this risk. Therefore, unless the damage is trivial, it is generally better for the racket to be replaced.

7.4.2 在决定是否允许运动员继续使用损坏的球拍时，裁判长必须首先考虑对手的利益。例如：尽管要求继续使用的运动员甘愿冒风险用损坏的拍面击出的球反弹可能不规则，这会增加双方击球的难度，然而除非损坏是轻微的，通常最好还是要求运动员更换球拍。

8 CLOTHING

8 服装

8.1 Colour

8.1 服装颜色

8.1.1 The main colour of clothing must be clearly different from that of the ball in use, but the “main” color does not necessarily mean the colour occupying the greatest area. A solid patch of color on the front of a shirt that covers only 40% of the area may still be the dominant colour, whereas a much larger percentage of same colour evenly dispersed could be relatively unnoticeable. The purpose of this clause is to ensure visibility of the ball, and for that reason the colour of the back of the shirt can be disregarded.

8.1.1 服装的主体颜色必须与比赛用球的颜色明显地区分开来，但“主体”颜色并不必一定是指覆盖区域最大的颜色，而短袖运动衫前面一块单一的颜色，虽然仅占整个衣服的40%，却仍是主体颜色。鉴于此，占很大比率的同一种颜色如果只是均匀分布，可能会相应地不被注意。这一条款的目的是保证球的可见性，因此运动衫后面的颜色可以不予考虑。

8.1.2 It is the apparent colour of the clothing, which is important, and the referee has to decide whether it provides sufficient contrast with the colour of the ball. Predominantly yellow clothing may be quite acceptable with an orange ball and patterned clothing having a white background may be satisfactory with a white ball, provided the perceived colours of clothing and ball are clearly different.

8.1.2 重要的是服装的明显颜色，裁判长必须确定它是否与比赛用球的颜色形成足够的反差。只要服装的颜色与比赛用球的颜色明显不同，穿黄色为主的服装可以打橙色比赛用球，穿底色是白色有图案的服装打白色比赛用球也可以被接受。

8.1.3 There are no specific restrictions on the color or size of badges, but they must comply with the normal requirements for the colour and design of clothing. On the back of the shirt players may wear lettering identifying themselves or their Associations or, in club matches, their club, and in this case white or any color may be used; such lettering must not obscure any identifying numbers that the organizers require a player to wear.

8.1.3 徽章的颜色和尺寸没有特别的限制，但是它们必须符合对服装颜色、设计的通常要求。在比赛服的背面可有表明该运动员、或其协会、或其俱乐部(在俱乐部比赛中)的白色或其他任何颜色的文字，但这些文字不得与主办方要求运动员佩戴的识别号码混淆。

8.1.4 Opposing players and pairs must wear shirts of clearly different colours. The umpire must resolve any question in this regard before the players start their practice period and, preferably, before the players arrive at the playing area.

8.1.4 双方运动员必须穿着颜色明显不同的服装。裁判员必须在运动员练习前，且最好在运动员到达比赛区域前解决这方面的问题。

8.1.5 An umpire who considers that the shirts worn by opposing players are not sufficiently different should ask them to decide which of them will change; if they do not accept his or her ruling the matter must be reported to the referee. Where it is decided that one must change and they cannot agree which will do so, the decision must be made by lot.

8.1.5 裁判员如果认为双方运动员的服装未能明显不同，则应要求他们自己决定哪一方更换服装。如果运动员不接受裁判员的裁定，裁判员应报告裁判长。如果决定一方运动员必须更换服装，但双方都不愿意更换，裁判员应主持抽签决定某一方必须更换。

8.1.6 The purpose of this regulation is to help spectators to distinguish between players, and the possible distance of spectators from the playing area must be taken into consideration. Colours which look quite different close-up can appear almost identical when seen from the back row of spectator seats, and opposing players' shirts should preferably be of different basic colors and not just different shades of the same color. This could also extend to the back of a player's shirt, especially in TV matches, where it is important that players are easily distinguishable. If a player has to change a shirt for any reason during a match the new shirt does not have to be the same colour as the one being changed, but still has to comply with the above clauses.

8.1.6 上述规程的目的是为了便于观众区分运动员，同时必须考虑到观众与赛区之间可能的距离。近看完全不一样的颜色，后排观众看起来可能几乎一样，因此双方运动员服装的基本颜色最好是明显不同，不应是同一种颜色的深浅不同。这一规定也可以延伸到运动员服装的背面，尤其是在电视转播的比赛中，重要的是运动员可以容易被区分。如果赛中由于任何原因运动员需要更换运动衫，新运动衫的颜色不必与被替换的颜色一样，但仍旧遵从上述规定。

8.2 Design

8.2 设计

8.2.1 Clothing may be of any design provided it does not bear symbols or lettering that might cause offence or otherwise bring the game into disrepute. The referee is responsible for determining what is and what is not acceptable for such reasons, but examples of markings which would be precluded are obscene pictures or lettering and political slogans or messages in any language.

8.2.1 一般来说，服装可以任意设计，但不得带有可能冒犯或诋毁本项运动声誉的符号或文字。裁判长有权决定哪些是可接受的，哪些是不可接受的，但必须排除淫秽的图案、文字和任何文字的政治标语及信息。

8.2.2 Players of the same Association forming a doubles pair in international competitions are allowed to wear clothes of different manufactures, if the basic colours are the same and their National Association authorises this procedure.

In a world, Olympic or Paralympic Title Competition players of the same Association must be dressed uniformly, with the possible exception of socks, shoes, and the number, size, color and design of advertisements on clothing (noting that no advertisements are allowed in Olympic and Paralympic competitions except for the clothing manufacturer) .

8.2.2 在国际比赛中，如果服装基本颜色相同，并获得所属协会的授权，同一协会的运动员组成的双打配对可以穿着不同制造商的服装。在冠名的世界、奥运会、残奥会的比赛中，同一协会的运动员必须穿着同样的服装，鞋、袜、服装上广告的数量、尺寸、颜色和设计可以例外（注意在奥运会和残奥会比赛中，除了服装制造商外不允许有广告）。

8.3 Advertisements

8.3 广告

8.3.1 Shirts, shorts or skirts may carry advertisements in addition to the logo or trademark of the maker of the garment, although advertisements for certain types of products are precluded. These advertisements are limited in size and number but may otherwise be of any design, provided that they are not so conspicuous or brightly reflecting as to unsight an opponent, and that they do not include offensive wording or symbols.

8.3.1 运动衫、短裤或短裙上除了有服装制造商的标志和商标外，可允许有广告，但某些产品的广告除外。服装上广告的尺寸、数量有限制，而设计没有限制。广告不得过于显眼或明显反光以至于影响对手视线，也不能有冒犯性词语或符号。

8.4 Legality

8.4 合法性

8.4.1 It is usually the umpire who first has the opportunity to consider whether players' clothing complies with the relevant regulations. If he or she is sure that it is illegal he or she should explain why to the player and, if the player accepts his or her decision and modifies or replaces the garment with one that is legal, no further action is needed. Only where the umpire is uncertain or the player does not accept the umpire's decision would the referee be consulted.

8.4.1 通常是裁判员最先有机会去考虑运动员的服装是否符合相关规定。如果他（她）确信运动员的服装不合法，应向运动员做出解释；如果运动员接受决定，改变或更换了不合法的服装，那么就没有采取进一步行动的必要。只有当裁判员不能确定或运动员不接受裁判员的决定时，才向裁判长请示。

8.4.2 It is often a matter of judgment whether clothing complies with the regulations and the referee's decision is final on any question of legality.

8.4.2 经常发生需要判断服装是否符合规定的情况，任何有关服装合法性的问题均由裁判长决定，裁判长的决定为最终决定。

8.4.3 Although it is reasonable to expect umpires to report any doubts about the legality of clothing, the referee should check for himself or herself, by looking round the playing hall from time to time, that there are no obvious failures to meet the required standards. This should be done as early as possible in a competition, as it is difficult to justify banning a garment, which has been accepted without question in several previous matches.

8.4.3 尽管裁判长等待裁判员报告可能存在的服装不合法的情况是理所应当的，但是裁判长应不时地巡视比赛大厅，亲自检查有无明显的不符合规则要求的情况。在比赛中，裁判长应该尽早地这样做，因为已经在先前比赛中被允许穿着的服装，再被禁止上场是很困难的。

8.4.4 In making decisions about the legality of clothing and other playing equipment, the referee must be consistent, both among players at the same competition and, as far as practicable, with the standards applied at other similar competitions. Where he or she is uncertain, he or she may be able to make a comparison with similar garments that have been accepted previously and conform to a more widely used standard.

8.4.4 对服装合法性和其他比赛器材的裁决，裁判长既要对同一场比赛的所有运动员，又要和其他类似比赛实施的标准尽可能地保持一致。在他（她）无法确定时，可以与先前得到认可的类似的服装进行比较，并遵守一个更广泛使用的标准。

8.4.5 The regulations define “normal clothing” but do not specifically preclude the wearing of such items as headgear and “cycling shorts”, and the referee must decide in each case what he or she will allow, taking into account presentation of the sport. Headgear worn for religious reasons and headbands to prevent long hair from obscuring a player’s view are clearly acceptable, but most referees would not allow the wearing of, for example, reversed baseball caps.

8.4.5 规程所定义的“普通服装”里没有特别排除诸如头饰和紧身衣服等服饰，每一种情形必须由裁判长来决定是否可以穿戴，并考虑到本项运动的展示。由于宗教原因戴头饰和因为头发太长戴上发带以免影响运动员视线，是可以接受的。但大多数裁判长不允许反戴棒球帽。

8.4.6 Some players wear cycling shorts, usually under normal shorts, as a means of keeping muscles warm, and this practice is generally accepted. It is recommended, however, that where such shorts are worn they should be of the same color as the normal shorts and, in any case, they must not carry any advertisements or other markings.

8.4.6 有些运动员为了让肌肉保暖，通常在运动短裤里面再穿紧身短裤，这种做法通常是可以接受的。然而，建议这类短裤必须与运动短裤的颜色一致，在任何情况下，不得有广告和其他的标记。

8.4.7 If a player protests that he or she is being unsighted by brightly reflecting jewellery or other items worn by an opponent the umpire should ask for the offending items to be covered or removed. If this request is refused the matter must be reported to the referee, whether or not the umpire supports the protest. The fact that the item has been worn in previous matches is irrelevant, and each case must be decided on its merits.

8.4.7 运动员佩戴的反光的首饰或其他物品，可能干扰对手视线，如果对手提出异议，裁判员应该要求运动员摘掉或遮盖住。如果要求被拒绝，不管裁判员意见如何，都应报告裁判长。在以往的比赛中，佩戴了该物品没有被异议的事实不能成为理由，裁判长必须根据每个事例的具体情况做出裁决。

8.5 Track Suits

8.5 长袖运动服

8.5.1 A player may not normally wear any part of a tracksuit during play but in some circumstances the referee may give permission for him or her to do so. Examples of such circumstances are extremely cold in the playing hall, with the consequent risk of muscle strain, or a leg disability or injury that the player prefers to keep covered. If a track suit is worn in play, it must comply with the requirements for playing clothes. A player with a physical disability, either in a wheelchair or standing, may wear the trousers portion of a tracksuit during play, but jeans are not permitted.

8.5.1 运动员一般不得穿着任何长袖运动服参加比赛，除非得到裁判长许可。如：比赛大厅非常冷，可能有拉伤肌肉的危险，或者运动员的腿有伤残而不愿暴露等情况。如果允许穿长袖运动服比赛，也必须符合运动服装的有关要求。轮椅组和站立组肢体残疾的运动员，在比赛中可以穿长运动裤，但禁止穿牛仔裤。

8.6 Changing

8.6 更换

8.6.1 Players should be discouraged from changing items of clothing in full view of spectators. If a player needs to change a playing garment because it is torn or wet through perspiration, he or she may be allowed to leave the playing area to do so during any authorized interval in play, accompanied by an official. The referee may give permission on each occasion or as a general dispensation to umpires before play begins.

8.6.1 应该劝阻运动员在观众看得见的地方更换服装。如果运动员的服装被撕破或被汗水湿透，必须更换，可允许其在工作人员的陪同下，于比赛间歇期间，离开赛场去更换服装。裁判长可在有人提出要求时给予批准，也可在比赛前将此权力委托给裁判员。

9 DEFINITIONS

9 定义

9.1 The laws governing play are preceded by a set of definitions. The main purpose of these definitions is to explain the significance of the main technical terms used in the laws, which may be different from the normal meaning of the words, but it should not be overlooked that they can often help also in the interpretation of laws to cover circumstances that are not dealt with specifically.

9.1 指导比赛的规则前面有一系列的定义，其主要目的是解释规则中那些可能与平常意思不同的主要技术术语的含义。但它们常常有助于理解那些在有些情况下没有特别阐明的规则的意思，这一点也不可忽视。

9.2 For instance, the definition of “to strike” the ball is “to touch it with the racket, held in the hand, or the racket hand below the wrist”. From this it follows that a player who drops his or her racket during a rally but attempts to return the ball by hitting it with the hand in which he or she had been holding the racket cannot make a good return, because he or she is not "striking" the ball according to the definition.

9.2 例如："击球"的定义为"用执拍手中的球拍或执拍手手腕以下部位触球"。按照这个定义，一个回合中，运动员的球拍掉了，如果他（她）试图用刚才拿球拍的手来击球将是不合法的。

9.3 For the same reason he or she cannot make a good return by throwing his or her racket at the ball, because the racket does not "strike" the ball if it is not held in the racket hand at the moment of impact. However, a player may transfer his or her racket from one hand to the other during play and strike the ball with the racket held alternately in either hand, because the hand holding the racket is automatically the "racket hand".

9.3 同样，运动员也不能把球拍扔出去击球，因为球拍一旦脱离执拍手就不能算作"击球"。然而，比赛中运动员可以左右手交替执拍来击球，因为拿着球拍的手就是"执拍手"。

9.4 It is essential to understand when the ball is considered as being "in play" because it is only during this time that a point, other than a penalty point, can be scored. The ball is in play from the last instant at which it is stationary on the palm of the server's free hand before being intentionally projected in service, and until the server has taken this action this instant is not defined.

9.4 理解什么时候球处于比赛状态是很有必要的，因为只有在这段时间里才能得分，罚分除外。发球时，球被有意抛起前静止在发球员不执拍手手掌上的最后一刻起进入比赛状态，之后发球员完成抛球动作。否则，并不表示球进入比赛状态。

9.5 Thus if the ball accidentally rolls off the server's hand before he or she starts to throw it his or her opponent does not score a point, because the ball was not in play. For the same reason a player may place the ball on his or her free hand and hold it stationary but then change his or her mind about the type of service he or she will make and move to another position to do so. Provided he or she has made no attempt to throw the ball, no point is scored.

9.5 因此，如果在发球员准备抛球前，球突然从其手中滑落下来，不判接发球方得分，因为球还未进入比赛状态。同样，发球员把球静止地放在不执拍手上，这时他（她）改变了主意，想换另一种发球，于是走到另一边去，也不判接发球方得分。只要他（她）没有试图抛球，就不判接发球方得分。

9.6 Once the ball is in play it remains in play until the rally has been decided as a let or point. The ball does not go out of play simply because it goes outside the playing area or above the level of the lights without touching them, but it does do so if it passes over a player's court or beyond his or her end line without touching his or her court since last being struck by his or her opponent.

9.6 球一旦进入比赛状态，这一状态一直持续到判定该回合为重发球或得分的情况为止。仅仅因为球飞离赛区，或者超过灯光但未触及灯光装置，则并不能认为球脱离比赛状态。对方击球后，该球未触及本方台区而越出本方台区或越过本方端线，则认为球已脱离比赛状态。

9.7 The intention of "obstruction" is that a player will be penalized under this law only if he or she intercepts the ball in a way that is likely to prevent an opponent making a good return. There is no obstruction if the interception occurs when the ball has passed beyond his or her end line, has passed outward over the sideline or is otherwise moving away from the playing surface.

9.7 关于"阻挡"：现行的规则规定，只有当运动员可能挡住了对方合法击出的球时才将被判为"阻挡"而罚分。如果此球已越过端线或边线并且不可能再落到台面时被拦住，就不算"阻挡"。

10 SERVICE

10 发球

10.1 Consistency

10.1 一致性

10.1.1 Consistent application of the service law always presents difficulties, perhaps because it has become so complicated, and there is sometimes a tendency for umpires to pay most attention to the aspects that they find easiest to check. To offset this tendency, the umpire should keep in mind the purpose of the various requirements and try to ensure that they are applied in a way that meets their objectives.

10.1.1 也许是由于多年来发球规则变得非常复杂，在裁判员中有一种自然倾向，即把注意力更多地放在那些他们认为是最容易检查的方面，因此裁判员对发球执法保持一致性就显得很困难。要消除这种倾向。裁判员应该牢记规则的总目的，并且努力保证在这个目的下执行规则。

10.2 Free Hand

10.2 不执拍手

10.2.1 The requirement for the server's free hand to be open is intended to ensure that the ball is not gripped in any way, so that the player cannot impart spin to the ball as he or she throws it. In applying the law the umpire should be less concerned with details such as the precise curvature of the server's free hand than with satisfying himself or herself that the ball is resting freely on its palm.

10.2.1 规则要求发球员的不执拍手张开，是要保证不能以任何方式握住球，以避免抛球时使球旋转。在执行时，裁判员的注意力不应放在诸如发球员不执拍手弯曲的确切程度的细节上，而应该注意球是否被随意地放在手掌上。

10.2.2 To help ensure that the ball can be seen resting freely on the palm it is required to be stationary above the level of the playing surface. The free hand may not be held stationary, dropped below the table surface and then brought upwards with a continuous sweep of the arm to throw the ball; if the hand is not brought to rest again above the level of the playing surface the service is illegal.

10.2.2 为了确保球被随意放在手掌上，规则要求：球必须静止地处于比赛台面之上。不执拍手不得由静止状态又下降到低于台面，再向上做连贯的挥臂抛球动作，如果不执拍手在高于比赛台面后没有停顿一下，这个发球就是不合法的。

10.2.3 The ball, but not necessarily the whole of the free hand, must also be behind the server's end line from the start of service until it is projected upwards. Thus a player may begin service with his or her arm and part of his or her free hand over the playing surface without being penalized, provided the ball itself is clearly behind the end line.

10.2.3 从发球开始到向上抛球，球必须始终位于发球员的端线之后，但不是指整个不执拍手。因此，发球时只要球明显地在端线之后，运动员的手臂或者不执拍手的部分在比赛台面上方，就不会被判发球违例。

10.3 Throwing The Ball

10.3 抛球

10.3.1 The server is required to throw the ball "near vertically" upwards and it must rise at least 16 cm after leaving his or her hand. This means it must rise within a few degrees of the vertical, rather than within the angle of 45° that was formerly specified, and that it must rise far enough for the umpire to be sure that it is thrown upwards and not sideways or diagonally. In Diagram 10.3.1.1services B and C are acceptable, whilst A and D are not. The height of the toss is also a factor in determining whether the toss is near vertical. In Diagram 10.3.1.2 the ball is projected from, and struck at, the same place, but service A is a fault, whilst B is acceptable.

10.3.1 发球员必须近乎垂直地向上抛球，并使球在离开不执拍手手掌后至少上升 16 厘米。这意味着球的上升只能在少数几个垂直角度内，而不是以前所允许的 45°角，并要高得使裁判员确信抛球是向上的，而不是向旁边或斜的方向。在图10.3.1.1 中，B 和 C 的发球是可以接受的，而 A 和 D 的发球则不合法。高度也是决定抛球是否垂直的一个因素。在图10.3.1.2 中，球从被抛起到击出在同一个位置，A 的发球是违例而 B 的发球可以接受。

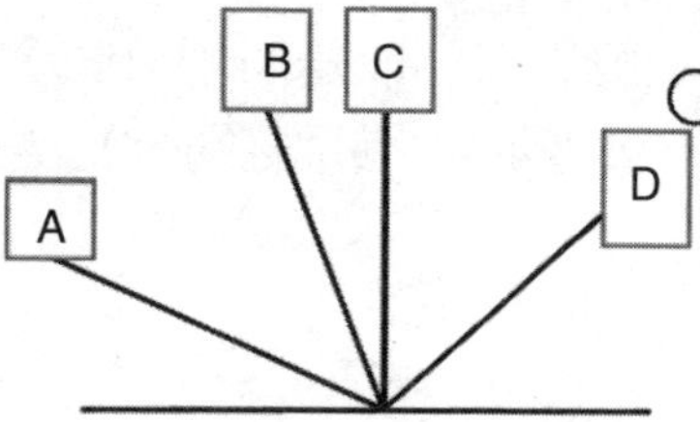

Diagram 10.3.1.1
图 10.3.1.1

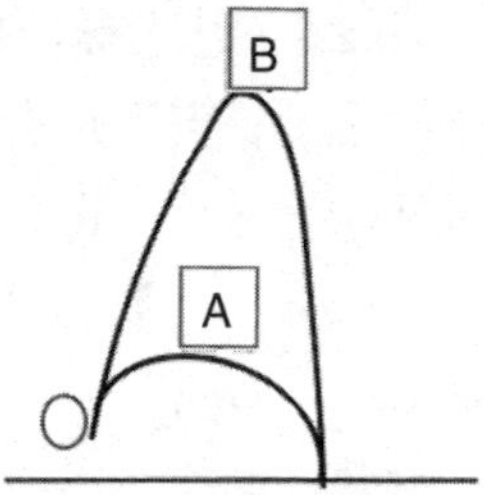

Diagram 10.3.1.2
图 10.3.1.2

10.3.2 The lower limit of 16cm is just greater than the height of the net, which provides a convenient reference.

10.3.2 16 厘米的最低限度正好比球网稍高，因此，网高就提供了一个便捷的参照物。

10.4 Striking The Ball

10.4 击球

10.4.1 The ball must not be struck until it is falling from the highest point in its trajectory. At the moment of contact with the racket the ball must be above the level of the playing surface and behind the end line.

10.4.1 当球从抛起的最高点下落时才能击球，击球点必须在比赛台面的水平面之上和发球员的端线之后。

10.5 Visibility

10.5 可见度

10.5.1 The primary requirement of the current service law is for the server to ensure that the receiver can see the ball throughout the service, and the umpire or assistant umpire must be satisfied that this is the case. The umpire or assistant umpire should look to see that the ball is not hidden from the receiver at any stage by any part of the body, or anything he or she or his or her doubles partner is wearing or carrying, and that the server's free arm, which includes the free hand, is moved from the space between the ball and the net, as soon as he or she releases the ball.

10.5.1 现行发球规则首先要求确保接发球员能看清发球的整个过程，裁判员或副裁判员必须确信这一要求被遵守。裁判员或副裁判员应注意观察在任何阶段，发球员身体的任何部分、或者发球员或其双打同伴穿戴或携带的任何物品都不能遮挡接发球员看球的视线，并且发球员的不执拍手臂包括不执拍手在抛球后，应立即从球和球网所形成的区域内移开。

10.5.2 The ball must be above the level of the playing surface at the start of service. There is, however, no specific requirement for the receiver to be able to see the racket throughout service, and the server may quite legitimately begin service with the racket concealed, for example, behind his or her back.

10.5.2 从抛球开始到击球，球必须始终高于比赛台面。然而，规则中并没有明确规定发球时要让接发球员看清球拍，因此，发球员可以在发球前将球拍合理地隐藏起来，如放在他（她）的身体背后。

10.5.3 From their positions in line with the net it may be impractical for the umpire and / or an assistant umpire to judge whether the ball is struck illegally if it is struck close to the end line or beside a player's body. It is, however, the responsibility of the player to serve so that the correctness of his or her service action can be seen and if he or she serves near the margins of illegality he or she runs the risk of being penalized.

10.5.3 如果击球靠近端线，或者靠近运动员的身体，那么要求裁判员或副裁判员以他们所处的与球网平行的位置来判断击球是否合法是不现实的。但是，运动员有责任让裁判员或副裁判员看清楚他（她）的发球是否合法，如果他（她）的发球接近不合法的边缘，他（她）就有被判罚的危险。

10.6 Warning

10.6 警告

10.6.1 An umpire or assistant umpire, who suspects, but is not sure, that a player's service action is illegal may warn the player without awarding a point. Only one warning may be given during a match and if any of his, or his or her partner's, subsequent services in that match is of doubtful legality, for the same or for any other reason, a point will be awarded to his or her opponent. A yellow card should not be used for a service warning.

10.6.1 当裁判员或副裁判员对运动员发球的正确性有怀疑，但不确定时，可以警告发球员而不予判分。但一场比赛只能警告一次，对该运动员或其双打同伴在该场比赛中的任何一次发球再有怀疑时，无论什么原因，均判接发球方得 1 分。发球警告不出示黄牌。

10.6.2 Either the umpire or assistant umpire can issue a service warning. A player can only be given one warning.

10.6.2 裁判员或副裁判员都可以对发球进行警告。对一名运动员只能给予一次警告。

10.6.3 Whether or not a formal warning is given there is no objection to a player whose service action is only marginally acceptable being advised informally, between rallies, by either the umpire or assistant umpire, that any deterioration could make it illegal. Contrary to popular belief, a player is not entitled to a warning for a first illegal service, and a clear failure to meet the requirements of the service law should always be penalized by the award of a point.

10.6.3 不管运动员是否受到过正式警告，不反对裁判员或副裁判员在回合之间，非正式地向运动员提出劝告：其发球有可能变成不合法。与通常的想法相反，只要运动员明显地没有符合合法发球的规定，即应判接发球方得 1 分，而不是第一次发球违例应给予警告。

10.6.4 The umpire or assistant umpire has no power to ignore an infringement of the service law because he or she does not believe that it gives the server any advantage and there is no justification for overlooking a first offence in the hope that it was a temporary lapse. The offence may be repeated at a critical stage of the match, and a player penalized then could justly protest that he or she had been given no earlier indication that the action was illegal.

10.6.4 裁判员或副裁判员无权忽视那些看来并不会给发球员带来任何好处的发球犯规，也没有理由以为这只是个暂时的失误而忽略运动员的首次犯规。在比赛的关键时刻，类似的犯规可能再次出现，而这时如果判罚，运动员就可能提出合理的抗议，因为先前没有被指出这样的发球是不合法的。

10.7 Exceptions

10.7 例外

10.7.1 The umpire may relax the requirements for a correct service if he or she is satisfied that that compliance is prevented by a physical disability. This will always be done for Class 1 and Class 2 players (refer Appendix H). The player's international classification card contains a section indicating any physical limitations that the player may have affecting compliance with the requirements of a correct ser vice e.g. where a player with disability is either not able to straighten his or her palm or does not have a hand, the player may serve with a curved palm or toss the ball from his or her stump.

10.7.1 如果确信运动员因身体残疾而无法遵守合法发球的规定，裁判员可以放宽要求。1 级和 2 级的运动员通常会发生此类情况（参见附录 H）。运动员的国际分级卡上注明了可能会影响遵守合法发球规定的任何生理缺陷。如一名残疾运动员手掌无法伸直或没有手掌，该运动员发球时可以手掌弯曲或从断肢处抛球。

11 A LET
11 重发球

11.1 Purpose
11.1 目的

11.1.1 The primary purpose of a let is to end a rally without awarding a point when something has happened which may affect the result of the rally, but there are other occasions on which it is necessary to suspend play temporarily. Such occasions may include the correction of errors in the score, the serving order or the ends at which the players are playing and the introduction of the expedite system when the time limit is reached.

11.1.1 重发球的主要目的是当某种可能影响到回合结果的情况发生时，终止该回合而不予判分。但另有一些情况也必须暂时中断比赛，如：纠正比分错误、发球次序或方位错误，以及时间到了要实行轮换发球法等。

11.2 Net Cord Service
11.2 发球擦网

11.2.1 The most common reason for a let is that the ball touches the net assembly while passing over it in service. Provided the service is good up to the point at which the ball touches the net, the rally is a let if the ball then touches correctly the receiver's court or if it is obstructed by the receiving player or pair; if it does not touch the correct court at all and is not obstructed, the receiver scores a point.

11.2.1 重发球最常见的原因是：发出的球在越过或绕过球网装置时，触及球网装置。如果合法发出的球，擦网后落在接球方正确的台区内，或被接发球方或其同伴阻挡，则判重发球。如果球不是落在正确的台区内，也未被阻挡，则判接发球方得 1 分。

11.2.2 When the ball touches the net during service, the umpire and assistant umpire wait until the ball touches the correct court and then make the appropriate call, rather than introduce an additional signal before the rally is over that may interfere with play. (See Appendix E - Recommended Hand Signals and Calls)

11.2.2 发球过程中球擦网，裁判员和副裁判员应等球落在正确的比赛台区，再喊“擦网”，而不是在回合结束前做出多余的手势，这会影响比赛。（见附录 E- 推荐的手势和宣告）

11.2.3 If either the umpire or the assistant umpire believes that the ball in service touches the net the rally is a let. Even if there is only a suspicion that the ball touches the net in an otherwise good service it is better to declare a let than to allow play to continue, because there is a risk that one or more players may have the same suspicion and, as a result, will be unable to give full attention to the course of play.

11.2.3 不管是裁判员还是副裁判员认为发球擦网了，都必须重发球。即使只是怀疑发球擦网，最好还是宣布重发球，而不要让比赛继续下去，因为总有一名或更多的运动员也同样怀疑擦网了，这样将影响他们全身心地投入比赛。

11.2.4 A player who believes that the ball touched the net in an otherwise good service may sometimes raise his or her arm or catch the ball and ask the umpire to declare a let. Unless the umpire is certain that it did not he or she will usually concur, especially if the server agrees with his or her opponent, but he or she should make clear that he or she is under no obligation to do so and that the player should continue playing if the umpire does not declare a let.

11.2.4 有时运动员认为合法发球擦网，会举起手臂或抓住球，要求裁判员判重发球。除非裁判员确信没有擦网，通常他（她）会判重发球，特别是当接发球方也认为是擦网时。但裁判员应让该运动员明白他（她）没有权力这样做，如果裁判员没有判重发球，运动员应该继续比赛。

11.3 Interruptions

11.3 中断

11.3.1 Another common reason for a let is a disturbance that may affect the outcome of the rally, such as a ball from another table coming into the playing area or a sudden noise which is sufficiently loud to startle the players. Here again, it is better to declare a let immediately if there is a risk of an interruption than to wait until the rally has ended and then to decide whether or not the disturbance was significant.

11.3.1 重发球的又一个常见原因，是认为某些干扰可能影响到回合的结果。例如：外界球进入赛场，或者是足以使运动员大吃一惊的突然喧闹。这种情况，也最好立刻宣判为重发球，而不要等到回合结束后再去判断干扰是否重要。

11.3.2 A let should not normally be declared for occurrences due to hazards which were present at the start of a rally. For example, a player who fails to make a good return because he or she collides with his or her doubles partner, or trips over a surround is not entitled to the benefit of a let, but one may be allowed if the incident disturbs the conditions of play in a way which could be disadvantageous to an opponent.

11.3.2 回合开始时偶然出现的不测事件，一般不应判为重发球。例如：运动员由于与同伴相撞（双打中）或者被挡板绊倒而未能合法还击，不能判重发球。但如果不测事件扰乱了比赛条件，可能对对方更不利时，可以判重发球。

11.4 Unreadiness

11.4 未做好准备

11.4.1 The umpire may declare a let if the receiver is not ready, provided he or she makes no attempt to return the ball. However, the fact that the receiver makes no stroke does not itself justify a let and the umpire must decide whether the receiver was really unready or, perhaps, merely unwilling to try to return what appeared to be a difficult service. Players should be encouraged to show when they are unready by raising a hand.

11.4.1 如果接发球员未做好准备，也没试图接球，裁判员可以判重发球。但是，接发球员未击球本身不能成为判重发球的正当理由，裁判员必须判定接发球员是确实没有准备好，还是只是不愿意接似乎是难接的发球。应当鼓励运动员在他们尚未做好准备时举手示意。

11.5 Wheelchair play

11.5 轮椅组比赛

11.5.1 If the receiver is in a wheelchair due to a physical disability, the rally is a let if the ball comes to rest on the receiver's court, or after touching the receiver's court returns in the direction of the net, or in singles, leaves the receiver's court after touching it by either of the sidelines. This is because a player in a wheelchair, by definition, is restricted in the extent of his or her ability to stretch and a service returning towards the net or going out from the sidelines is regarded as unfair. The ball can cross the sideline after one or more bounces. However, in singles play and where the ball is traveling towards the side line, if the receiver strikes the ball before it crosses a sideline or takes a second bounce on his or her side of the playing surface, the service is considered good and no let is called.

11.5.1 如果接发球员因身体残疾而坐轮椅，如果球停在接发球方的台区，或在触及接发球方台区后向球网方向返回，或在单打比赛中在触及接发球方台区后，从任意一侧边线离开接发球方台区，回合应被判为重发球。这是因为根据轮椅运动员的定义，他（她）的伸展能力受到限制，如果发出的球朝着球网方向返回或从边线处离开球台是不公平的。球可以弹跳一次或多次越过边线。然而，在单打比赛中，当球向边线方向运行时，如果接发球方在球越过边线或在本方台区内第二次弹起前将球击出，该球被认为是合法发球，不判重发球。

12 A POINT

12 一分

12.1 Decision

12.1 判定

12.1.1 Each rally that is not a let results in the award of a point and the laws specify the various reasons for which a point is scored. The decisive stage of a rally is usually that at which the ball goes out of play and the umpire should beware of making a decision based on what he or she expects to happen, without allowing for the possibility that the rally may be ended in some quite different way which may invalidate his or her decision.

12.1.1 每个回合除重发球外必须判分，规则规定了判分的各种不同的依据。一个回合的关键通常在于球脱离比赛状态的那一时刻，裁判员应该谨防根据自己的预测来做出判定，因为该回合可能以完全不同于他（她）预测的结果而结束。

12.1.2 For instance, the ball may be returned by a player, well wide of the table, so that it is clear that it will not touch the opponent's court; but the rally does not end until the ball goes out of play and either player may still win the point. If, in these circumstances, the opponent moves the playing surface while the ball is in play, it is the player who struck the wide return who wins the point, even though the return was unlikely to be good.

12.1.2 例如，球可能被运动员击得离开球台很远，很显然不会触及对方的台区，但该回合要到球脱离比赛状态才结束，双方运动员都还有可能得分。上述事例中，如果对方使比赛台面移动，把球打飞的那个运动员将得分，即使他的回球不可能是合法还击。

12.1.3 Not all points are scored for reasons directly related to play, such as the failure to make a good service or a good return. For example, if while making a potentially winning hit a player accidentally touches the playing surface with his or her free hand or moves the table while the ball is in play, his or her opponent will score a point, whether or not he or she is likely to be able to make a good return.

12.1.3 不是所有的失分都像未能合法发球或合法还击那样直接与比赛有关。例如，当一名运动员打了一个制胜的球，但球尚未脱离比赛状态时，他（她）的不执拍手不小心触及了比赛台面或移动了球台，对方运动员将得 1 分而不再考虑对方能否合法还击。

12.1.4 The umpire must never award points for reasons that are not supported by the laws, perhaps because he or she considers that one player “deserves” a point or that another should be penalized for an unfair action. The umpire should always be able to justify any decision he or she makes by reference to a law and it is for this reason that he or she should study carefully and understand all of the reasons for which a point may be scored.

12.1.4 裁判员决不能在规则规定条文以外判分，例如：他（她）认为由于某个不正当的行为，一名运动员应该被奖励 1 分，而另一名应该受罚。裁判员的所有判决总是应该有相应的规则依据，因此，他（她）应该仔细研究、理解所有可以判分的规则条文。

12.1.5 Some infringements of the laws or regulations do not automatically stop play and the umpire may have to do so by calling the score. In some cases it will be obvious to the players why the rally has ended; where it is not obvious the umpire or assistant umpire should be ready to explain the reason for his or her decision. He or she may be able to do so by means of signs or by using one of the standard terms of explanation (18.4.2).

12.1.5 某些犯规并不自动导致停止比赛，必须通过裁判员的报分来终止。回合为何被终止，运动员有时清楚，有时可能不清楚，裁判员或副裁判员应该解释判决的理由，可以用手势或使用规范的术语进行解释（18.4.2）。

12.1.6 A player who is in a wheelchair due a physical disability and who does not maintain a contact with the seat or cushion with the rear side of at least one of the thighs just before striking the ball is considered to be gaining an unfair advantage and the opponent is awarded a point.

12.1.6 由于身体残疾而坐轮椅的运动员，如果在击球前，至少一只大腿的后部未能与轮椅座位或坐垫保持接触，该运动员会被认为不公平获利，判对方得 1 分。

12.1.7 If a player is in a wheelchair due to a physical disability, he or she may only touch the table with his or her racket hand to restore balance, only after a shot has been played, provided the playing surface does not move. The player is not allowed to use the table as an extra support before striking the ball. Similarly the player may not use his or her free hand on the table as an extra support, or touch the playing surface at any time during the rally. In a doubles match this applies to both players.

12.1.7 由于身体残疾而坐轮椅的运动员，只有在击球后才可以用执拍手接触球台以恢复身体平衡，并且不能移动比赛台面。不允许运动员在击球前利用球台获得额外支撑。同样的，运动员也不可以将自己的非执拍手放在球台获得额外支撑，或在回合的任何时间触及比赛台面。这也同样适用于双打比赛中的双方运动员。

12.2 Edge Balls

12.2 擦边

12.2.1 It is necessary to decide whether a ball which touches the edge of the table makes contact on or below the playing surface, and the path of the ball before and after it touches the table can help the umpire or assistant umpire to arrive at the correct decision. If the ball first passed over the playing surface the return is good, but if it touched while it is still rising from below the level of the playing surface, it almost certainly touched the side.

12.2.1 当球触及球台的边缘时，必须认定球是触及比赛台面的上沿还是下沿，球触及球台的前后路线轨迹可以帮助裁判员做出正确判断。如果球首先是从台面上方越过，则认为还击是合法的；若球是从台面下方上升期触及球台，则几乎肯定球触及的是下沿（侧面）。

12.2.2 The main difficulty arises when a ball arrives from outside, and above the level of, the playing surface, and here the best guide is the direction of the ball after contact with the table. There is no infallible guide but, if, after touching the edge, the ball travels upwards, it is reasonable to assume that it touched the playing surface but, if it continues downwards, it is more likely to have touched the side.

12.2.2 当球是从高于比赛台面的上方且从台外向台内飞行时，这时认定就比较困难，这里最好的指引是看球触球台后的飞行方向。当然，没有永远正确的指引，如果球触球台后仍然向上，则有理由推断球触及了比赛台面，但如果球触及球台后向下，则很可能是触及了下沿(侧面)。

12.2.3 The assistant umpire is solely responsible for edge ball decisions at the side of the table nearest to him or her. If he or she believes that the ball touched the side he or she should call "side", and the umpire must award a point to the opponent(s) of the last striker. Only the umpire can decide on edge balls at the ends and at the side nearest to him or her.

12.2.3 副裁判员全权决定处于比赛状态中的球是否触及距离他（她）最近的比赛台面的上沿。如果他（她）确信球触及了球台侧面，则喊“侧面”，裁判员应判最后一板击球方的对手得 1 分。只有裁判员才有权决定处于比赛状态的球是否触及两条端线和距离他（她）最近的比赛台面的上沿。

12.3 Doubt

12.3 怀疑

12.3.1 An umpire who is certain that he or she has made a correct decision should not change it simply because the players think he or she is wrong, but he or she may appear officious if he or she insists on maintaining a decision with which both players or pairs strongly disagree. There is also a risk that the player who benefited from the decision may then deliberately fail to make a good service or return, and this will diminish the umpire's authority.

12.3.1 裁判员肯定自己所做的判定是正确的，就不应该仅仅因为运动员认为是错的而进行改判。但是，如果他（她）坚持自己的判定，而双方运动员都强烈反对该判定，他（她）就显得太自负了。如果他（她）这样做，由此受益的运动员就可能故意失 1 分来表示反对，这只能削弱裁判员的权威。

12.3.2 A decision should never be reconsidered solely at the request of the player who would benefit from a change, even if his or her opponent offers no objection, and a request for reconsideration should be ignored once another rally has started. Exceptionally, where both players or pairs are sure that a decision is wrong and the umpire can accept that he or she may have been mistaken, he or she would be wise to accept the correction.

12.3.2 决不考虑仅由一名运动员提出的改判要求，而该运动员可能因改判而受益，即使对方不反对，一旦下一个回合开始，不允许提出改判要求。除此之外，如果双方运动员都坚持认为判定是错误的，则裁判员可以接受并理智地加以纠正。

12.3.3 When there is a genuine doubt in the mind of the umpire he or she should give the benefit of the doubt to the player who may have committed an offence, provided he or she is certain that an opponent has not been adversely affected. If, however, there is a risk that a player's attention has been distracted during the play because he or she too suspected that his or her opponent infringed a law but was not penalized, the rally should be declared a let.

12.3.3 如果裁判员心里确实有怀疑时，在肯定对方不会受到不利影响前提下，他（她）应该让那一名可能犯了规的运动员继续打下去。如果存在一名运动员因为也怀疑对方犯规却没受判罚而导致注意力分散的可能性，该回合应该判为重发球。

13 CONTINUITY OF PLAY

13 比赛的连续性

13.1 Time-out

13.1 暂停

13.1.1 In addition to the statutory intervals between games, each player or pair, or their captain or adviser on their behalf, is entitled to claim a time-out period of up to 1 minute during an individual match. Making a T-sign with the hands indicates the request, which can be made only between rallies after the start of the game.

13.1.1 除了法定的局与局之间的间歇外，一名或一对双打运动员或队长或指导者可在一场单项比赛中要求一次暂停，时间不超过 1 分钟。请求暂停只有在一局比赛开始后的回合之间做出，应用双手做出“T”形表示。

13.1.2 On receiving the request the umpire should suspend play and hold up a white card, raising the arm above the head, on the side of the player or pair making the request. The assistant umpire should then place a special signboard (or a white marker) on the court of the player or pair making the request. After placing the special signboard (or white marker) and before removing it from the table, the assistant umpire shall stand beside his or her table. Play is resumed when this player or pair is ready to do so, or at the end of 1 minute, whichever is the sooner. The special signboard (or white marker) should then be removed from the table and a white marker be placed near the score indicator, next to the score of the player or pair who requested the time-out. If an umpire is working without an assistant, he or she should show the white card, and, if it can be done easily, place a special signboard (or white marker) on the court of the player or pair making the request.

13.1.2 在得到一方暂停的请求后，裁判员应暂停比赛，手臂高举过头，向要求暂停一方的一侧出示白牌。然后副裁判员将特殊标志牌（或白色标志物）放在提出要求暂停一方运动员的台区上。从特殊标志牌（或白色标志物）放置到球台上到被移走前，副裁判员应站立在自己的裁判桌旁。当提出暂停的一方运动员准备继续比赛，或 1 分钟暂停时间到（以时间短的计算），应立即恢复比赛。拿走特殊标志牌（或白色标志物），并在翻分器旁要求暂停一方运动员的得分处放置白色标志物。如果裁判员独自一人执裁，则应该出示白牌，并且如果容易的话，将特殊标志牌（或白色标志物）放在提出要求暂停一方运动员的台区上。

13.1.3 If a captain / adviser and a player / pair disagree whether a time-out is to be taken, the captain has the final decision in a team match and the player / pair in an individual match.

13.1.3 如果队长 / 指导者和一名运动员 / 一对运动员对是否要求暂停有不同意见，在团体比赛中，队长或指导者对暂停有最终决定权；在单项比赛中，运动员有最终决定权。

13.1.4 If both players / pairs ask for a time-out at the same time, the time allowed is still up to 1 minute but they need not return earlier unless both players / pairs are ready to resume. Neither player / pair is entitled to another time-out in that individual match.

13.1.4 如果双方运动员同时提出暂停，暂停时间仍为 1 分钟，并且除非双方运动员都回来才继续比赛。在该场比赛的剩余时间里，任何一方都不得要求再次暂停。

13.2 Time-wasting

13.2 拖延比赛

13.2.1 The requirement is for play to be continuous throughout a match, apart from authorized intervals, but if, for example, the ball goes outside the playing area, clearly play cannot continue until it is returned. The intent of the regulation is to prevent deliberate time-wasting, such as by repeated bouncing of the ball, long pauses before serving and prolonged discussions with a doubles partner, which should be firmly discouraged.

13.2.1 除了规定的休息和批准的暂停以外，规程规定一场比赛必须连续进行。如果球飞出场外，显然比赛不能继续，需要一点时间去捡球。保持比赛连续性的目的是为了防止诸如重复拍球，发球前长时间的停顿、双打时长时间相互讨论等故意拖延比赛时间的行为，此类行为应坚决劝阻。

13.2.2 Players are not allowed to receive advice or instructions from their coaches or advisers after practice. They may practice for up to 2 minutes, but as soon as they have finished they must start play, even if the practice period has lasted for less than 2 minutes.

13.2.2 运动员在赛前练习 2 分钟后，不允许再接受教练员或指导者的指导。练习时间为 2 分钟，一旦练习结束，即使真正练习的时间不到 2 分钟，比赛也必须立即开始。

13.3 Towelling

13.3 擦汗

13.3.1 It is the duty of the umpire to ensure that any interruptions are as short as is practicable and that players do not take advantage of any concessions to gain extra rest periods or disturb the rhythm of an opponent's play. The pace of modern table tennis, especially when played in warm conditions, makes occasional breaks for toweling necessary but such breaks are now limited to specified stages of play.

13.3.1 裁判员有责任让任何比赛中断时间尽可能地短暂，运动员不得利用任何中断时间而获得任何额外休息或打乱对方的节奏。现代乒乓球比赛的节奏，尤其是在炎热的条件下比赛，经常须中断比赛来擦汗，但是，现在规定了擦汗只能在比赛的某些阶段进行。

13.3.2 Players are entitled to brief breaks for towelling after every 6 points from the start of a game, and at the change of ends in the last possible game of a match. Spectacle wearers can have particular problems, especially in hot conditions, and the umpire may allow them short breaks for cleaning between any rallies.

13.3.2 只有在每局比赛开始后每 6 分或者决胜局交换方位时才允许短暂的擦汗。戴眼镜者可能有其特殊的麻烦，尤其在炎热的环境中，因此，裁判员应允许他们在回合之间用短暂的时间擦拭眼镜。

13.3.3 The purpose of the restriction on toweling is to prevent it being used as a delaying tactic, either to gain extra rest time or to disturb the rhythm of an opponent's game. There is no reason why players may not towel at times which do not further interrupt the continuity of play, such as when the ball is being retrieved from outside the playing area, but care must be taken that players do not deliberately cause such breaks.

13.3.3 对擦汗的限制，目的在于防止把擦汗作为一种拖延战术来利用，以便获得额外的休息，或者打乱对方的比赛节奏。没有理由不允许运动员在并不延长比赛中断时间的情况下擦汗，例如，当球飞离赛区去捡回时。但是，必须注意运动员是无意识地制造这样的中断。

13.4 Damaged Equipment

13.4 器材的损坏

13.4.1 Another possible reason for an interruption of play is damage to playing equipment. No interval can be allowed for a player to fetch a new racket if the one he or she is using is damaged, because he or she is required to be able to replace it in the playing area. If he or she replaces a racket and this racket also becomes damaged the umpire must report to the referee, who will decide how a second replacement is to be provided.

13.4.1 比赛中断的另一种可能原因是比赛器材的损坏。如果比赛中运动员的球拍损坏，不允许中断比赛去取新球拍，而应要求运动员在比赛区域内更换。如果这块球拍又损坏，裁判员必须报告裁判长，由裁判长决定如何进行第二次更换。

13.4.2 Replacement of a damaged ball should not be allowed to hold up play unduly, but players should be allowed a few practice strokes with the new ball before resuming play.

13.4.2 不允许花费过多的时间来更换破裂的比赛用球，但是允许运动员在重新比赛前用新球练习几次。

13.4.3 The failure of a light, or other serious disturbance of the playing area, that could cause delay should be re ported immediately to the referee, who may transfer the match to another table if one is available.

13.4.3 发生灯光损坏或其他可能延误比赛的严重干扰时，应立即报告裁判长，裁判长在可能的情况下，可将比赛调换到另一张球台上进行。

13.5 Injury

13.5 受伤

13.5.1 If, owing to accident or illness, a player is unable to continue the umpire must report immediately to the referee. The referee may authorize an emergency suspension of play for the player to receive treatment or to recover by resting, provided he or she is satisfied that the break in continuity will not unfairly affect an opponent and that the player will be able to resume play within a reasonably short time. The timekeeper should time the suspension from the time when the referee is called, not from the time he or she arrives at the playing area.

13.5.1 比赛中，运动员发生意外或生病不能继续比赛，裁判员应立即报告裁判长。裁判长可允许紧急中断比赛，让运动员接受治疗或休息片刻，只要他（她）确信中断比赛不会给对方带来不利，并且运动员能在合理的短时间内恢复比赛。计时员应从报告裁判长的那一刻开始计算中断时间，而不是从裁判长到达比赛区域的那一刻开始计时。

13.5.2 No interval can be allowed where the disability is due to illness or unfitness that was present or to be expected at the start of the match, or to effects such as exhaustion resulting from the way in which play has proceeded. If an interval is granted, it should be as short as possible and not longer than 10 minutes, but if anyone in the playing area is bleeding, play must not be resumed until all traces of blood have been removed.

13.5.2 如果运动员因为疾病或身体不适而失去比赛能力的状况早已存在，或在比赛开始时就有理由可以预见，或由于比赛的进行方式引起过度疲劳，则不允许中断比赛。如果比赛获准中断，中断的时间要尽量短些，不得超过 10 分钟。但如果赛区内有人受伤流血，应直到赛区内的所有血迹擦干净后再恢复比赛。

13.5.3 Once a player has been granted an interval for recovery from injury, normally he or she should be allowed no further such interval during that match. Exceptionally, where the first interval was very short, another brief interval may be allowed for treatment provided that it is not likely to be prejudicial to the opponent and that the total period for which play is suspended during the match does not exceed 10 minutes.

13.5.3 运动员一旦获准利用中断时间进行受伤后的恢复，那么通常在该场比赛中，他（她）不能再要求类似的中断。除非首次中断的时间非常短，再次短暂中断接受治疗不会给对方带来不利，才可允许再次中断比赛，而且一场比赛中总的中断时间不能超过10分钟。

13.5.4 If a player with a disability is unable to play temporarily due to the nature of his / her disability or condition, the referee may, after consulting a medical classifier or doctor at the competition, allow a medical recovery time of the shortest practical duration, but in no circumstances more than 10 minutes

13.5.4 如果残疾运动员因残疾或身体条件的原因而暂时丧失比赛能力，裁判长在征询医学分级师或赛会医生的意见后，可以允许最短可行的医疗恢复时间，但任何情况下都不得超过10分钟。

13.6 Leaving Playing Area

13.6 离开赛区

13.6.1 Players must normally remain in or near the playing area throughout an individual match, except with the permission of the referee; during intervals between games and time-outs they shall remain within 3 metres of the playing area under the supervision of the umpire.

13.6.1 在单项比赛中，运动员必须留在赛区或赛区附近，除非得到裁判长的许可；在局与局之间和暂停的间歇时间，运动员在裁判员的监督下留在赛区 3 米以内的区域。

13.7 Rest Periods

13.7 休息时间

13.7.1 Players should not be allowed to extend the intervals between games and should be called back if they have not returned at due time. Each interval is limited to 1 minute and if players do not take all the time available to them at one interval they may not claim extra time at the next. It is not necessary for the players or pairs to agree on taking a rest period, which must be allowed if any player wishes to take one.

13.7.1 局间休息时间不允许延长，如果休息时间结束时运动员尚未回到比赛球台，应将其召回。所有的局间休息都是 1 分钟，一次局间休息时间没有用完不能移加到下一次。任何一方都可以要求局间休息，不必征得对方的同意。

14 ORDER OF SERVING, RECEIVING AND ENDS

14 发球、接发球和方位的次序

14.1 Choice

14.1 选择

14.1.1 At the start of a match the choice of serving, receiving and ends is decided by lot, usually by tossing a coin or disc having two distinct sides. The player who wins the right to choose first may decide to serve or to receive first or to start playing at a particular end of the table. If he or she decides to serve or receive first his or her opponent has the right to choose an end and vice versa, so that both players have a choice to make.

14.1.1 一场比赛开始前，发球、接发球和方位的选择由抽签决定，通常使用掷硬币或两面颜色不同的挑边器。中签运动员可以首先选择发球或接发球，或选方位。如果他（她）选择先发球或先接发球，对方就选择方位，反之亦然。因此，双方都有一次选择。

14.1.2 In each game of a doubles match, the pair due to serve first may choose which of them will serve first and in the first game the opposing pair must then decide which of them will receive first. In subsequent games the striking order is defined by the initial order, which reverses for each game. When first one pair scores 5 points in the last possible game of a match, the receiving pair must change their order of receiving.

14.1.2 在双打比赛中，每局首先发球的一方可以决定他们中谁先发球，该场比赛第一局的接发球方可以决定他们中谁先接发球。在以后的各局中，按开始时确立的次序击球，并逐局互换。决胜局中一方先得 5 分时，接发球方应交换接发球次序。

14.1.3 In a doubles match between A, B and X, Y, the only two possible orders of striking are A-X-B-Y-A-.. and A-Y-B-X-A-.., but the sequence may start with any player, depending on the choices made at the start of each game.

The umpire should note the striking order at the start of the match and of the first server in each game, so that any errors can be corrected by reference to the appropriate starting point.

14.1.3 在A、B对X、Y的一场双打比赛中，只有两种击球次序：A-X-B-Y-A……和A-Y-B-X-A……，但次序可由4名运动员中的任何一名开始，根据每局比赛开始所做的选择而定。裁判员应记录下比赛开始时的击球次序和每一局的第一发球员，以便发生错误时能参照开始时的次序进行纠正。

14.1.4 When a doubles pair comprises two players who are in wheelchairs due to a physical disability, the server first makes a service and the receiver makes a return, but thereafter either player of the disabled pair may make a return. However if any part of a player's wheelchair protrudes beyond the imaginary extension of the centre line of the table, the umpire will award a point to the opposing pair. This also applies when a "mixed" pair (one standing and one wheelchair) are playing together. Either player may return the ball (after initial service and return), but each player has to remain in his or her own half of the court. No part of the player's wheelchair can cross the imaginary extension of the centre line and the standing player cannot put a foot over this line either.

14.1.4 由于身体残疾而坐轮椅的运动员组成的双打，发球员首先发球，然后接发球员还击，随后双打配对中的任何一位都可以还击。然而如果运动员轮椅的任何一部分越过了球台中线的假设延长线，裁判员将判对方得1分。这同样也适用于“混合”（一位站立和一位轮椅）配对的比赛。在发球和接发球后，双打配对中的任何一位都可以还击，但是每一位都必须保持在自己的半区。轮椅运动员的任何一部分都不得越过球台中线的假设延长线，站立运动员的脚也不能越过这条线。

14.2 Errors

14.2 错误

14.2.1 The correction of errors in striking order or ends is based on two principles. First, as soon as the error is discovered, play is stopped and is resumed with the correct order or ends; second, any points that have been scored while the error persisted count as though it had not occurred. If an error is noticed during a rally the umpire should immediately declare a let, and not wait until the ball is next out of play.

14.2.1 发球、接发球和方位错误根据两条原则来纠正：首先，一旦发现错误，立即中断比赛，按正确的次序和方位继续比赛。其次，错误发现前的比分有效。回合进行中，一旦发现错误，裁判员应立即判重发球，而不要等球成结束比赛状态再宣判。

14.2.2 The score that has been reached usually determines who should be serving and receiving but if, in doubles, the pair who should have served first in a game did not do so, the umpire cannot know which of them would have served first. If this happens he or she should ask them immediately who would have been their first server, and he or she can then calculate the order in which play will resume.

14.2.2 通常可由场上比分来确定该谁发球、谁接发球。但在双打中，假如一局比赛应该首先发球的一方没有先发球，裁判员就无法弄清该谁先发球。如果这样的事情发生了，裁判员应立即要求这对运动员决定谁是第一发球员，然后计算出次序，继续比赛。

15 EXPEDITE SYSTEM

15 轮换发球法

15.1 Principle

15.1 原则

15.1.1 The expedite system is the method provided by the laws to prevent unduly long games, which may result from negative play by both players or pairs. Unless 18 in total have been scored it is introduced automatically after 10 minutes' play in a game or at any earlier time at the request of both players or pairs.

15.1.1 轮换发球法是防止由于比赛双方消极防守导致比赛时间过于长久的一种方法。如果一局比赛 10 分钟仍未结束，则自动实行轮换发球法，除非双方比分相加至 18 分；或在此之前应双方运动员的要求实行轮换发球法。

15.1.2 Under the expedite system the serving player or pair has 13 strokes including the service stroke in which to win the point. If the receiving player or pair safely makes 13 good returns, the receiving player or pair wins the point. The game is won, as in normal play, by the player or pair first scoring 11 points or, if the score reaches 10-10, by the play er or pair first establishing a lead of 2 points.

15.1.2 实行轮换发球法，发球方必须在包括发球一板在内的 13 次击球中取胜。如果接发球方合法还击 13 次，则接发球方得分。同正常比赛一样，一局比赛先得 11 分的运动员获胜。10 平后，先多得 2 分的一方获胜。

15.1.3 The serving order throughout each game is the same as for a normal game, but service changes after each point instead of after every 2 points. At the start of each game the first server, and in doubles the first receiver, is determined by the order established at the start of the match, even though the same players may have been serving and receiving at the conclusion of the preceding game.

15.1.3 实行轮换发球法，每局的发球次序同正常比赛一样，只不过是每 1 分交换发球，而不是每 2 分才交换。每局比赛开始谁先发球、双打比赛中谁先接发球，均由该场比赛开始时建立起来的次序来确定，即使发球员、接发球员可能与前一局结束时的运动员相同。

15.2 Procedure

15.2 程序

15.2.1 When the time limit is reached, unless 18 points have been scored, the timekeeper should call “Time” loudly. The umpire should then declare a let if necessary and tell the players that the remainder of the match will be conducted under the expedite system. If the ball is in play when the time limit is reached, the next server is the player who served for that rally; if it is not in play, the next server is the player who received in the preceding rally.

15.2.1 当时限到时，除非比分已达到 18 分，计时员应大声宣告“时间到”。如有必要，裁判员应宣布暂停并告诉运动员该场比赛的剩余部分将实施轮换发球法。如果时限到时，球处于比赛状态，则该回合为重发球，由该回合原来的发球员先发球；如果时限到时，球处于非比赛状态，则由前一回合的接发球员先发球。

15.2.2 Thereafter, in each rally the stroke counter is required to count aloud the return strokes of the receiving player or pair, including the return of service, from "one" to "thirteen". The call should be made immediately after the receiver has struck the ball and not delayed until the return has been judged good or the ball has gone out of play. If the 13th return is good the umpire should call "stop" and award a point to the receiver.

15.2.2 此后，在每个回合，计数员都必须大声报接发球方的还击次数，从接发球开始，从"1"数到"13"。当接发球方击球后应立即报数，不要等球成为合法还击或球脱离比赛状态后再报数。如果第 13 次还击是合法还击，裁判员应喊"停"，并判接发球方得 1 分。

16 ADVICE TO PLAYERS

16 场外指导

16.1 A player may receive advice during the intervals between games or during any other authorized suspension of play, but not between the end of practice and the start of play, during breaks for toweling or while he, or his or her opponent, is retrieving the ball.

16.1 运动员可在局间休息时间或其他经批准的中断时间

内接受场外指导，而在赛前练习结束到比赛开始前、擦汗时、运动员或其对手捡球时不得接受场外指导。

16.2 In a team event he or she may receive advice from anyone authorised to be at the playing area but in an individual event he or she may receive advice from only one person, who must be nominated to the umpire before the match. Where a doubles pair consists of players from different Associations, each may nominate an adviser. These advisors are treated as a single unit for the purposes of the advice regulations. A single warning applies to both, and if either of the pair gives advice illegally after either has been warned, both would be sent away from the playing area.

16.2 在团体比赛中，运动员可以接受有权进入比赛区域的任何人的指导，但在单项比赛中只能接受一个人的指导，而这位指导者的身份应在赛前向裁判员说明。由不同协会的运动员组成的双打配对，可分别授权一位指导者。在有关场外指导的规程上这两位指导者应被视为一体，一位被警告视为另一位也受到了警告，如果一位被警告后另一位进行了非法指导，那么两位指导者都将被逐出比赛区域。

16.3 When anyone tries to give advice illegally the umpire should first warn him or her by holding up a yellow card so that it is clearly visible to everyone concerned, but there is no need for him or her to leave his or her chair to do so. In a team match, such a warning applies to everyone on the "team bench". If in that team match anyone again gives advice illegally, the umpire should hold up a red card and send that person away from the playing area. Another advisor cannot replace an advisor who is sent away from the playing area for giving advice illegally.

16.3 当有人非法指导时，第一次，裁判员应出示黄牌警告非法指导者，并让每一个有关人员都能看清楚，但裁判员没有必要走下裁判椅去出示黄牌。在团体比赛中，一人被警告视为教练员席上的其他人也都被警告。如果有人再进行非法指导，裁判员应出示红牌并将其逐出比赛区域。因非法指导被逐出比赛区域的指导者不能被另一名指导者替代。

16.4 A dismissed adviser must go far enough away to ensure that he or she cannot influence play. In an individual event he or she may not return until the match ends; in a team event he or she may not return until the end of the team match except to play, when he or she may return only for the duration of his or her individual match. If he or she refuses to leave or returns before he or she is entitled to do so the umpire should suspend play and report to the referee.

16.4 被逐出的指导者应远离赛场，确保不再影响比赛。在单项比赛中，直到比赛结束，他（她）才能返回比赛区域。在团体比赛中，比赛没结束时他（她）也不能返回比赛区域，除非轮到他（她）上场比赛。如果他（她）拒绝离开比赛区域或在比赛未结束前返回比赛区域，裁判员应中断比赛并报告裁判长。

16.5 Attempts may be made to advise a player by calling out to him or her during play, but the umpire must becareful to distinguish between advice and shouts of encouragement. Advice need not be spoken and hand signals are often used; this type of advice is difficult to detect, as is advice given in an unfamiliar language, but match officials must be alert to any illegal attempt to influence play and act promptly to deal with it.

16.5 在比赛中，指导者有时可试图通过叫喊来指导运动员。裁判员必须仔细区分是指导还是激励性叫喊。应该记住，指导不一定非用语言不可，通常可以用手势来进行。这种形式的指导，如同用不熟悉的语言指导一样很难察觉，但是，比赛官员必须警惕任何试图影响比赛的违例行为，一经发现，应即行处理。

16.6 The "behaviour" regulations include provision for use of the penalty point system to control advice given illegally, but its application should be limited to situations where it is clear that it is the player who is seeking advice. It would be unfair to penalize a player for simply receiving advice that he or she has not sought and may not want and in most cases it is better to deal directly with the illegal adviser.

16.6 在规程中有关"行为"的条款包括了使用罚分系统来控制非法指导，但只有在很明显是运动员主动寻求不合法的场外指导时才能使用。对于运动员并没有主动寻求，可能也不想要的非法指导而判罚运动员是不公平的。在大多数情况下，最好是直接处理非法指导者。

16.7 The assistant umpire may often be in a better position than the umpire to see that advice is being given illegally. If advice is given illegally the assistant umpire should immediately draw this to the umpire's attention, interrupting play if necessary by calling "stop" and raising his or her hand. The umpire should then take any appropriate action.

16.7 副裁判员所处的位置通常可能比裁判员更方便观察到非法指导。如发生非法指导，副裁判员应立即让裁判员注意这一行为，必要时可举手喊“停”来暂停比赛。裁判员这时应采取适当的纪律行动。

17 BEHAVIOUR

17 行为

17.1 Responsibility of the Umpire

17.1 裁判员的职责

17.1.1 Deliberately unfair or offensive behaviour is not common in table tennis and is usually limited to a small minority of players and coaches, but its effects may be very damaging and it is often difficult to control. Because misbehaviour can take many forms, it is impractical to lay down precise rules, and setting and applying acceptable standards of conduct is more a matter of judgment and common sense than of factual decision.

17.1.1 故意的不公正或冒犯行为在乒乓球比赛中并不普遍，通常只发生在少数运动员和教练员身上，但其影响却非常大，并且常常难以控制。因为不良行为形式多样，因而制定确切的规则来限制是不现实的，且制定和实施切实可行的行为标准，与其说是根据事实做出判定，不如说是一个判断和常识问题。

17.1.2 The umpire should be ready to respond immediately to any sign that bad behaviour by a player or coach is likely to be unfair to an opponent, to offend spectators or to bring discredit to the sport. If he or she tolerates early lapses in good behavior, however trivial, without even a disapproving glance he or she will find it much harder to impose proper discipline if these lapses later become more persistent or serious.

17.1.2 对运动员和教练员任何可能不公平地对待对方运动员，或者冒犯观众，或有损本项运动声誉的行为迹象，裁判员应迅速做出反应。如果裁判员宽容了最初的哪怕是轻微的不良行为，甚至连不赞同的目光都没有，那么，如果以后这样的行为变得更多或更严重，再采取相应的纪律行动就会很困难。

17.1.3 The umpire should, however, avoid over-reaction to possibly unintentional instances of unseemly behaviour, for this could lead to resentment and animosity that will undermine his or her authority. When he or she takes action he or she should always try to do so in a way that does not make the situation worse, either by drawing undue attention to an incident that may not have been generally noticed or by appearing to victimize a player or coach.

17.1.3 但是，裁判员也不要对那些可能不是故意的不当行为反应过激，因为这会导致不满和敌意，从而有损于自己的权威。在处理这类事件时，裁判员要设法不让情况变得更糟，不要过分注意一般不会觉察到的事件或者不要表现得会伤害运动员或教练员。

17.1.4 An example of behaviour which might justify action by the umpire is shouting during play, in annoyance or elation, but in deciding how to react the umpire should take account of the environment in which it occurs. If the general noise level is so high that the player's shouting is hardly noticeable, it is more sensible not to stop play but to wait until the end of the rally before speaking to the offending player.

17.1.4 例如，比赛中大声叫喊，不管是高兴还是恼怒，裁判员应对这种不良行为采取行动，不过在处理时应该考虑行为发生时的环境。如果场上喧闹声很大，运动员的叫喊几乎不引人注意，最好不要中断比赛，而应等到该回合结束后再向该运动员提出。

17.1.5 Another example of bad behaviour is gross disrespect of match officials by players or coaches, usually to demonstrate disagreement with a decision. This may take the form of persistent protest, alteration of the score indicators or even threats against the officials. Such behavior detracts from the presentation of the sport and from the authority of the match officials, and must be strongly resisted.

17.1.5 另一个不良行为的例子是运动员或教练员对裁判员不尊重，通常是不同意裁判员的判决。他们采取的行动包括坚持抗议、改变翻分器上的比分，甚至恐吓裁判员等。像这类严重诋毁本项运动精神和裁判员权威的不良行为必须强烈抵制。

17.1.6 When misbehaviour occurs, the umpire has to decide whether the offence is so serious that he or she must suspend play and report immediately to the referee. Although this option is always available and should be used when appropriate, it should rarely be necessary on the first occasion and in most circumstances the initial action should be to give the offender a warning.

17.1.6 当发生不良行为时，裁判员必须确定其是否严重到必须中断比赛并立即报告裁判长。虽然这种选择是可取的并在适当时可以采用，但在首次情况下很少需要这样做，大多数情况下应该先警告冒犯者。

17.1.7 The assistant umpire may often be in a better position than the umpire to see misbehaviour. If this occurs the assistant umpire should immediately draw this to the umpire's attention, interrupting play if necessary by calling "stop" and raising his or her hand. The umpire should then take any appropriate action.

17.1.7 副裁判员所处的位置通常可能比裁判员更方便观察到不良行为。如果出现不良行为，副裁判员应立即请裁判员注意，必要时可举手喊“停”来暂停比赛。裁判员这时应采取适当的纪律行动。

17.2 Warning

17.2 警告

17.2.1 Unless the incident is so seriously unfair or ob jectionable that formal action cannot be avoided, a quiet informal word of warning or even a warning signal should be sufficient to make the offender aware that such behaviour is unacceptable. Wherever possible, this should be done without interrupting play, taking advantage of the next natural break such as the end of the rally or the end of the game.

17.2.1 除非不良行为非常不当或引起反对而必须采取行动，一声轻轻的非正式警告语，甚至一个手势，就足以使运动员醒悟自己的行为是不可取的。尽可能地不中断比赛，利用下一次自然间歇的机会，如回合结束时或一局结束时提出。

17.2.2 When, however, the umpire believes that an opponent may have been adversely affected or that the behavior is likely to offend spectators or otherwise to be detrimental to the sport he or she should immediately declare a let and formally warn the offender, by holding up a yellow card, that further misbehaviour will incur penalties.

17.2.2 如果确信对方运动员被不良行为所影响或不良行为可能冒犯了观众或甚至诋毁了本项运动，裁判员应立即判重发球，并出示黄牌正式警告冒犯者，如果再次冒犯将被判罚分。

17.2.3 When a formal warning has been given, a yellow marker should be placed near the score indicator, next to the score of the player who has been warned. Similarly if a player has had a penalty point awarded against him or her, both a yellow and red marker should be placed near the score indicator, if space permits. If both the umpire and assistant umpire are using score indicators then the cards should only be placed on the assistant umpire's indicator. These warning apply for the remainder of the individual match or, in a team event, the remainder of the team match, and subsequent offences will incur penalty points.

17.2.3 当运动员受到正式警告，一张黄色标志物将放在翻分器该运动员得分旁。同样地，运动员如被罚分，一张黄色和红色标志物将同时放置在翻分器该运动员得分旁，如果翻分器旁有足够的空间。裁判员和副裁判员同时使用翻分器时，这些标志物只能放置在副裁判员的翻分器处。这些警告在本场单项比赛的剩余时间内一直有效，在团体赛中还将带到该场团体赛剩余的比赛中。再次冒犯将被判罚分。

17.2.4 It should be remembered that, once a formal warning has been given, subsequent offence must automatically be penalized by the award of points. The umpire should not be afraid to use this procedure when it is justified, but if a formal warning is given too readily he or she may find that he or she has to penalize a player at a critical stage of a match for an offence that to many people may appear trivial.

17.2.4 应当记住，一旦给予了正式警告，随后的冒犯就要被判罚分。只要是正当的，裁判员就不要害怕使用这个处罚程序，但如果正式警告给得太随意了，裁判员可能会发现自己不得不在一场比赛的关键阶段，对运动员的一个在许多人看来并不严重的冒犯行为进行罚分。

17.3 Penalties

17.3 判罚

17.3.1 If a player who has been formally warned commits a further offence in the same match the umpire should award 1 penalty point to his or her opponent and for a third offence he or she should award 2 points, each time holding up a yellow and a red card together to show the action he or she has taken. Should misbehaviour continue after the umpire has imposed these penalties he or she should suspend play immediately and report to the referee.

17.3.1 如果运动员受到正式警告后在同一场比赛中再次冒犯，裁判员应判对方得 1 分；第 3 次冒犯，判对方得 2 分。每次罚分，裁判员都应同时出示红牌和黄牌。如果在裁判员已进行了这些判罚后，运动员仍有冒犯行为，裁判员应立即中断比赛，报告裁判长。

17.3.2 When the umpire awards a penalty point, the referee should be advised as soon as practicable, but without delaying play, to enable the referee, if he or she wishes, to come to the playing area so that he or she will be readily available in case of any further trouble. If the referee or his or her deputy is not in a position to see the display of cards it may be possible to use another pre-arranged signal or to send a messenger.

17.3.2 裁判员实施判罚分，应尽快通知裁判长，但比赛应继续进行，目的是使裁判长能够亲临现场，以便事态进一步恶化时能及时处理。如果裁判长或副裁判长所在的位置看不见裁判员出示的牌子，应使用另一种事先约定的信号或派人送口信。

17.3.3 Penalty points may sometimes be awarded after a game has ended, or 2 penalty points might be awarded against a player when his or her opponent needs only 1 point to win the game. If the match has not ended any "unused" points are transferred to the next game of that individual match, so that it starts at the score of 0-1 or 0-2 in favor of the offender's opponent, but if the match has ended they should be ignored. In this case the server is the one who should have been serving at that score according to the sequence established at the beginning of the match.

17.3.3 有时候判罚分是在一局比赛结束后，或者判罚 2 分时对手只需 1 分就赢得这局比赛了。如果本场比赛还未结束，这些“未用的得分”将带到下一局比赛，即比赛一开始就是0:1或0:2，冒犯方的对手领先；但如果这场比赛结束了，这些得分就不必理会了。在上述例子中，应根据比赛开始时建立的次序，按场上当时的比分来确定发球员。

17.3.4 In a team match, warnings and penalties are carried over to subsequent individual matches. A doubles pair is regarded as having incurred the higher of any warnings or penalties incurred by either of the players; thus if one has been warned in a previous match and the other had incurred 1 penalty point, a first offence by either of them in the doubles match would incur 2 penalty points. A warning or penalty during a doubles match applies to the pair during that match, but only the offending player will carry it over to a subsequent individual match. The following example illustrates this point: In a team match with 4 singles and 1 doubles matches, players A & B are paired to play the doubles match. In their first singles matches in this team match, A was warned and B incurred a penalty point. In the 2nd game of the doubles match A intentionally breaks the ball by stepping on it. The umpire awards 2 penalty points against A / B. In their next singles matches, each player carries forward 1 penalty point.

17.3.4 在团体比赛中，运动员受到警告或判罚将带到其随后的同一场团体赛的单打比赛中。双打运动员中任一名在同一场团体赛中已经受到的最严重的警告或判罚应视作该对双打运动员的。因此，如果双打运动员中的一名在前一场比赛中受到警告，另一名受到1分的判罚，则在双打比赛中任何一人第一次冒犯，将被判罚 2 分。在双打比赛中受到警告或判罚应被视作该对运动员的，但只有冒犯的那名运动员才会将这些警告或判罚带到同一场团体赛的单打比赛中。举例如下：在由 4 场单打和 1 场双打组成的团体比赛中，A 和 B 配对打双打。在团体比赛各自的第一场单打比赛中，A 受到警告，B 被判罚 1 分。在双打比赛的第二局中，A 故意踩破球，裁判员判 A / B 失 2 分。在随后的单打比赛中，A 和 B 各带 1 分的判罚。

17.3.5 In a team match it is necessary to record warnings and penalties so that they can be transferred to later matches, but it is advisable to do so also in individual events. This will allow the referee to take account of persistent bad behaviour when deciding, for example, whether to disqualify a player. The record can conveniently be a note on the score card, stating who was warned or penalized and at what stage of the match, with a brief description of the offence. This recording of warnings should also be applied to coaches for similar reasons.

17.3.5 在团体比赛中，有必要记录下运动员受到的警告或判罚，这样，这些判罚将带到本场团体比赛随后的单打比赛中。在单项比赛中这样做也是可取的，可以帮助裁判长考虑持续的不良行为是否很严重，例如是否要取消运动员的比赛资格。警告或判罚可以很方便地记录在记分单上，注明是谁被警告或被判罚以及在比赛的哪个阶段，并附上对冒犯行为的简短描述。同理，对警告的记录也适用于教练员。

17.3.6 It is clearly impracticable to award penalty points against a coach, and it would be unfair to award them against a player on whose behalf he or she may be protesting. If after a formal warning a coach continues to misbehave he or she should be shown a red card and sent away from the playing area until the end of the match or, in a team event, of the team match; where this action is taken the incident should be reported to the referee.

17.3.6 对教练员的不良行为进行罚分是明显地不切实际，因教练员的不良行为而对该方运动员进行罚分是不公平的，会引起运动员的抗议。教练员在受到正式警告后，如果在同一场单项比赛或团体比赛中再次冒犯，裁判员应出示红牌并将其驱逐出赛区，直到该场团体赛或单项比赛结束才可返回。采取这样的行动应报告裁判长。

17.4 Responsibility of the Referee

17.4 裁判长的职责

17.4.1 The referee may disqualify a player from a match, an event or a whole competition, depending on the gravity of the offence. This is a matter for his or her judgment but when a player is reported for continuing to misbe have after the award of 2 penalty points the referee would normally disqualify him or her, holding up a red card. In very serious cases he or she would also make a formal report to the player's parent Association.

17.4.1 裁判长可根据运动员冒犯行为的严重性，取消该运动员在一场、一项或整个比赛的资格。裁判长应自己判断，通常情况下如果运动员在被判罚 2 分后继续冒犯，裁判长将出示红牌取消其比赛资格。对于某些非常严重的事例，裁判长也可写报告给该运动员的所属协会。

17.4.2 Usually the referee learns of instances of bad behaviour from the umpire, but he or she may sometimes be able to see them and to take action before the umpire has invoked his or her attention. He or she can also anticipate possible problems by, for example, watching at least part of any match involving a player who has previously been warned or penalized for bad behaviour, to make sure that such behaviour does not continue.

17.4.2 一般来说，裁判长是从裁判员那里了解到不良行为的表现的，但有时他（她）也能亲自观察到，并在裁判员报告之前进行处理。他（她）也可以预测可能出现的问题，例如通过观看至少部分有因不良行为曾被警告或被判罚的运动员参加的比赛，以确信这种不良行为不会继续。

17.4.3 Even where there has been no previous incident it may be obvious from the reaction of spectators that one or more of the players in a match are misbehaving. By watching the match the referee may find that the umpire is no longer in control of play and in this situation he or she should take action on his or her own initiative, either by telling the umpire what he or she must do or by dealing directly with the offending player.

17.4.3 即使没有先前的事例，当比赛中有一名或更多的运动员出现了不良行为，通常可以明显地从观众的反应中觉察到。通过观看比赛，裁判长可能会发现裁判员无法继续控制比赛局面的情况，而这时，他（她）应该主动进行处理，或者告诉裁判员该怎样做，或者直接处理冒犯者。

18 MATCH CONDUCT

18 比赛管理

18.1 Score Calling

18.1 报分

18.1.1 The umpire should call the score clearly, taking care that the tone of his or her voice does not suggest partiality towards one player or pair; he or she may place a slight emphasis on the number of points which has changed as a result of the rally. If he or she is using a microphone he or she may need to adjust his or her speaking level, and / or the position of the microphone, and he or she should remember that it may well cause remarks that were not intended for the public to be generally audible.

18.1.1 裁判员报分应清晰，注意语调不要偏向某一方，对一个回合结束后比分发生变化的数字可稍微加重语气。如果使用麦克风，他（她）需要调整说话的音量或麦克风的位置，应记住麦克风可能会将他(她)并不想让观众听见的话也传出去。

18.1.2 The score should normally be called as soon as the rally has been decided and the umpire should not wait until he or she judges that the players are ready to resume play. However, if there is loud applause or a player is retrieving the ball from the back of the playing area he or she may prefer to delay his or her call slightly until he or she is satisfied that both players or pairs will be able to hear it.

18.1.2　一个回合结束时，裁判员通常应立即报分，而不必等到判断双方运动员准备继续比赛时再报。然而，如果喝彩声大或有一名运动员到赛区后捡球，可暂缓报分，直到确信双方运动员都能听见比分时再报。

18.1.3　The umpire should call first the number of points scored by the player or pair due to serve next, then the number of points scored by the opposing player or pair. At a change of service he or she should point to the next server. This may be followed by the name of the next server. Whether or not to name the server should be covered at the referee's briefing, with the main aim being that all umpires at an event act consistently. At the start of a game the server's name should be announced first.

18.1.3　报分时，应先报下一回合将要发球方的得分，再报对方的得分。换发球时，应用手指向发球方，也可以报出下一发球员的名字。是否报出发球方的名字由裁判长在赛前短会上决定，目的是使一次比赛所有的裁判员行为一致。一局比赛开始时，应先报发球方的名字。

18.1.4　Whilst it is optional for the umpire to use the players' names, he or she should be sure how to pronounce players' names correctly. The umpire should verify correct pronunciation before the match is started.

18.1.4　裁判员可报运动员的姓名，并正确地报出。为此应在比赛开始前求证运动员姓名的正确发音。

18.1.5　When each player or pair has scored, say, 4 points the score may be called either as "4-4" or "4-all"; the score 0 may be expressed as either "zero" or "love". At the start of a game the umpire should announce " Smith to serve", " Love all" or " Zero-Zero", to avoid the risk of players starting before the call is complete. If the rally is a let the umpire should repeat the existing score, to confirm that no point has been scored.

18.1.5 如果双方都得 4 分，可报为“4 比 4”或“4 平”，比分 0 可以用“0”或“love”来表示。一局比赛开始，裁判员应报“×××发球”，“0 比 0”或“love-all”，以避免报分未结束运动员已开始比赛。如果是重发球，裁判员应重报原有比分，以示该回合未得分。

18.1.6 In a team match the name of the Association may be used instead of, or as well as, the player's name. It is, however, a requirement to point to the next server. Thus in a team match between France and Poland, the opening announcement could be "Kinski of Poland to serve, 0-0". During an individual game the score might be called as " 6-4, France" and the announcement after an individual match could be "Game to Poland 11-6, Poland wins by 3 games to 0; Poland leads by 1 match to 0".

18.1.6 在团体比赛中，可以用比赛协会的名称替代运动员的名字，或者另加上运动员的名字来报分，但都要求指向下一发球方。例如：在法国队与波兰队的一场团体赛中，开赛可以报为“波兰队金斯基发球，0 比 0”；赛中比分可报为“6 比 4，法国”；一场比赛结束，其结果可报为“11 比 6，波兰队胜，波兰队以 3 比 0 胜该场比赛；波兰队 1 比 0 领先”。

18.1.7 In an international competition both the score and, when the expedite system is in operation, the number of strokes must normally be called in English, but a different language may be used by agreement between the umpire and both players or pairs. Other announcements should be made in English unless it is clear that another language is more ac ceptable to spectators.

18.1.7 在国际比赛中，通常必须使用英语来报分和报轮换发球法中的击球板数，如果裁判员和双方运动员都同意，也可以使用其他语言。除非观众显然更愿意接受另一种语言，其他方面的宣告应使用英语。

18.1.8 See Appendix F for Field of Play Procedures

18.1.8 见附录 F 临场操作程序

18.2 Signals

18.2 手势

18.2.1 In addition to calling the score the umpire is recommended to use hand signals to indicate certain decisions, especially where the noise level makes it difficult for a strokes call to be heard. Even if the umpire delays his or her call to allow for a burst of applause to subside or a player to return from retrieving the ball, a prompt signal will allow score indicators to be updated without having to wait for the score to be announced.

18.2.1 除了报分外，裁判员也可以用手势来表示判决，特别是在赛场喧闹声太大，运动员、观众及其他人员听不清裁判员的报分时。即使裁判员考虑等到掌声消退或运动员捡球回来时再报分，一个快速的得分手势也可以使比分更新而不必非得等到比分报出。

18.2.2 The umpire must point with his or her hand to

the next server at a change of service. He or she may also indicate the award of a point by raising the arm nearer to the player or pair who won it, so that the upper arm is horizontal and the forearm is vertical, with the closed hand upward. If he or she declares a let or wishes to delay the resumption of play he or she should raise one hand above his or her head, and the assistant umpire should use the same signal to attract the umpire's attention when he or she makes a decision within his or her jurisdiction. Hand signals should be clear and positive but they must not be unnecessarily flamboyant or aggressive.

18.2.2 换发球时，裁判员必须用手势指向下一个发球方。当判得分时，可将靠近得分方的手臂举起，上臂水平，前臂垂直，手握拳向上。如果要判重发球或希望推迟比赛，应将手高举过头。副裁判员在其权限内所做的判定需要引起裁判员的注意时也应使用同样的手势。手势应干净利落，不要带有夸张或挑衅意味。

18.2.3 See Appendix E for examples of correct hand signals and recommended calls by the umpire and assistant umpire during match situations.

18.2.3 正确的手势示例和推荐裁判员、副裁判员在比赛进行中使用的宣告方式参见附录 E。

18.3 Time Keeping

18.3 计时

18.3.1 The timekeeper must time the practice period, intervals between games and any authorized suspension of play. During a game, the timer should be stopped during significant breaks in play and re-started as soon as the next rally begins. Examples of such breaks are pauses for towelling; the change of ends in the last possible game of a match and delays while the ball is being retrieved from outside the play ing area. Retrieving the ball while still in the playing area is not a reason to stop the timer.

18.3.1 赛前练习、局与局之间的间歇及任何经批准的中断必须计时。一局比赛中，计时器在比赛中断时应停表，并在下个回合开始时重新开动，这些中断诸如擦汗、决胜局交换方位、捡回飞出赛区的球。在赛区内捡球不必暂停计时器。

18.4 Explanations

18.4 解释

18.4.1 It is not usually necessary to have to explain umpiring decisions, and announcements should be avoided. For example, if a player serves the ball into the net he or she has clearly not made a good service and there is no need to call “fault”. If, however, the rally is decided in a way that does not automatically end play or which may not be obvious a brief explanation may be given, using standard hand signals and / or the standard terms listed below.

18.4.1 通常，裁判员没有必要对判决做出解释，并且应避免不必要的宣告。例如，运动员发球下网，很明显未能合法发球，因此没有必要喊“犯规”。但是，如果一个判决并不能自动中止比赛或运动员、观众对该判决不清楚，则可以用标准的手势或下列标准术语予以简单解释。

18.4.2 The recommended explanatory terms are,

service not good	"fault"
net touched by player, clothing or racket	"touched net"
playing surface moved	"moved table"
free hand touched playing surface	"hand on table"
ball obstructed by player	"obstruction"
ball touched same court twice	"double bounce"
ball deliberately struck twice by same player	"double hit"
ball struck by wrong player in doubles	"wrong player"
in doubles service, ball touched wrong half-court	"wrong side"

18.4.2 标准解释术语如下：

发球不合法	"违例"
运动员身体、衣服或球拍触网	"触网"
比赛台面移动	"台面移动"
不执拍手触及比赛台面	"手触台面"
球被运动员阻挡	"阻挡"
球连续两次触及同一台区	"两跳"
同一运动员有意连续两次击球	"连击"
双打运动员击球次序错误	"次序错误"
双打发球时，球触及错误的半区	"错区"

18.4.3 A fuller explanation should be given if necessary-for instance, where a service has been ruled illegal and the player is not sure which of the requirements he or she failed to meet. Language problems can often be overcome by the use of signs, such as pointing to the edge of the playing surface if a player has not noticed that the ball touched it, or demonstrating an aspect of service action that has been penalised.

18.4.3　必要时应该进行详细解释，尤其是当运动员被判发球不合法且不清楚自己错在哪里时。语言障碍常常可以用手势来克服，如当运动员未注意球擦边时，用手指向球擦边处，或演示部分发球违例动作。

19　SCORE INDICATORS

19　比分显示器

19.1　The score is usually displayed on one or more score indicators. The correct use of score indicators is an important element in the presentation of a match and the umpire should make sure that the officials operating them are aware of their duties. Operators must await the umpire's call or signal before changing the score and must never anticipate decisions that they do not have the authority to make.

19.1　通常有一个或几个比分显示器显示比分。比分显示器的正确使用是比赛面貌的一个重要方面，裁判员应该使显示员明确自己的职责。显示员必须等裁判员报完分或做出手势后才显示比分，决不能抢在裁判员的判分之前预先判定，因为他们并无这种权力。

19.2　Most score indicators have two sets of large numbers to show the points scores and two smaller sets of numbers for the games scores. These indicators can provide a great deal of useful information, provided they are used con sistently. Before a match the games score indicators should be left blank and not set to 0 until both players or pairs arrive in the court, as a guide to whoever is controlling the programme of play.

19.2 目前，大多数比分显示器用两套大数字显示比分，用两套小数字显示局分。如果比分显示器使用一致，它可以提供许多有用的信息。比赛开始前可以把局分显示成空白，待双方运动员都到达比赛区域后再显示为“0”，为比赛进度的控制者提供参考。

19.3 Before a game starts the points score indicators should be blank, and should not show “0-0”; this score should be displayed only when the umpire calls it to announce the start of the game. At the end of a game the indicators should be left showing the final points score until just before the start of the next game, for the benefit of spectators, be fore being returned to the blank position.

19.3 一局比赛开始前，显示器上不应显示任何比分，只有当裁判员宣布比赛开始，报分后才显示 0 比 0 的比分。一局比赛结束后，为了方便观众，应在比分还原前，将比分保留一会儿，直至下一局比赛开始。

19.4 In no circumstances should the result of a game be shown simultaneously on the points and games score indicators. The games score should not be changed until the final points score in that game is reset so that, for example, until shortly before the start of the 4th game of a match the indicators may show a games score of 1 to each player and a points score of 11-7, but not 2-1 and 11-7.

19.4 任何情况下，一局比赛结果的比分与局分都不应同时显示在显示器上。直到该局比赛的比分还原后，才可以调整局分。例如，在第 4 局比赛开始前，显示器上局分应显示为

1∶1，比分显示为11∶7；而不是局分2∶1，比分11∶7。

19.5 Score indicators are normally placed in front of the umpire or assistant umpire, or both, facing towards the players, and in this position it is often difficult for spectators seated at the ends of the playing area to see them. The operator may rotate it by up to 45° to his or her left and / or right at suitable intervals during play, such as at a break for towelling or when retrieving the ball from the rear of the court, or at change of service. Provided the score indicator is reasonably light, and the operator feels it is necessary to do so, the operator may also raise the score indicator whilst ro tating it.

19.5 比分显示器一般放置在裁判员或副裁判员的前面，或两者前面都放，面向运动员。这个位置对于坐在赛场两端的观众来说，经常难以看清楚比分。显示器操作员可以在赛中合适的间歇时间，如运动员擦汗、去远处捡球、换发球时将比分显示器向左和 / 或右旋转45°。如果比分显示器重量较轻，显示器操作员认为必要，也可以将比分显示器边举起边旋转。

19.6 Most mechanical score indicators can display points scores up to about 20 and rarely will the score in a game exceed this figure. If this stage is reached one possibility is to reset them to 0∶0, but this can be confusing for spectators when they see the server changing after every point and it is generally better to revert to 10-10, a score at which the alternation of service is expected.

19.6 大多数机械显示器可以显示比分到20，很少有一局比赛的比分超过这个数字。一旦比分真的超过 20，一种可能是将比分复位到“0∶0”，但这会引起观众的困惑，因为他们看见的是每分交换发球；通常更好的办法是将比分调到“10∶10”，这符合每分交换发球。

19.7 See Appendix A for examples of the correct use of score indicators.

19.7 翻分器的正确用法参见附录 A。

20 CONCLUSION

20 结论

20.1 Whether working alone or as part of a team, the work of match officials can be difficult and demanding. They must be fair but not indulgent, firm but not officious and confident without being obtrusive. For most people these qualities are acquired only through experience, but it is hoped that the guidance given in this booklet will be of assistance to all those seeking to improve their competence as match officials.

20.1 无论是单独执法还是作为整个裁判队伍的一部分，裁判员的工作难度和要求均是很高的。他们必须具备公正而不迁就、严格而不多管闲事、自信而不自负等优良品质。对大多数人来说这些品质只有通过实践才能获得，希望这本小册子提供的指导对那些想提高比赛执法能力的人有所帮助。

Appendix A——Recommended Procedure for Match Officials

附录A——比赛官员操作程序（推荐）

1 Before going to the playing area, check that you have all the necessary equipment, such as net gauge, disc or coin for tossing, balls, score card, stop-watch and colored cards. Make sure that you understand how to complete the score-card.

1 在到达比赛区域前，检查比赛所必需的器材是否带齐，诸如量网尺、挑边器或硬币、比赛用球、记分单、秒表及红、黄牌等，并确信你已知道如何完成记分单的填写。

2 If possible, before entering the field of play make sure that team players, and doubles pairs of the same Association, are similarly dressed and that opposing players or pairs are wearing shirts of clearly different colours; report any non-compliance that you cannot resolve, or any doubt about clothing or rackets, to the referee.

2 如有可能，在进入比赛区域前确保团体比赛的队员、同一协会的双打配对服装穿着类似，并且比赛双方的服装颜色明显不同。出现不符合规则规定而裁判员无法解决的问题，或对服装或球拍有疑问，应报告裁判长。

3 On arrival at the playing area, check that the table and surrounds are correctly positioned and that the net is properly adjusted for height and tension. If a microphone is to be used, if practical make sure that it is working properly

and that you know the correct voice level.

3 到达比赛区域后，检查球台和挡板是否摆放正确，球网的高度及张度是否已调整好。如果使用麦克风，确保它能正常工作并了解它的正确音量。

4 Set the indicators to the blank position that is, so that they show no points or games scores (Figure 1). In a team match, check that the match score indicator is set correctly. When both players or pairs arrive in the court, set both games score indicators to "0" (Figure 2).

4 将比分显示器调到空白的位置，即显示无比分和无局分的状态（图 1）。在团体赛中，检查场分显示器是否设置正确。当双方运动员到达赛场后，将双方局分调至"0"（图 2）。

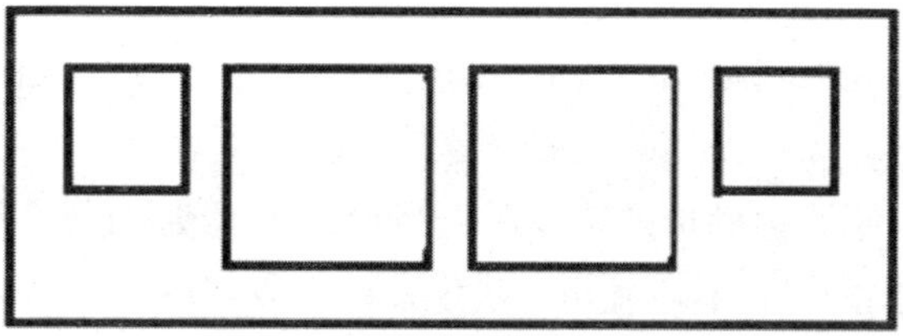

Figure 1: Before players arrive
图 1 运动员到场之前

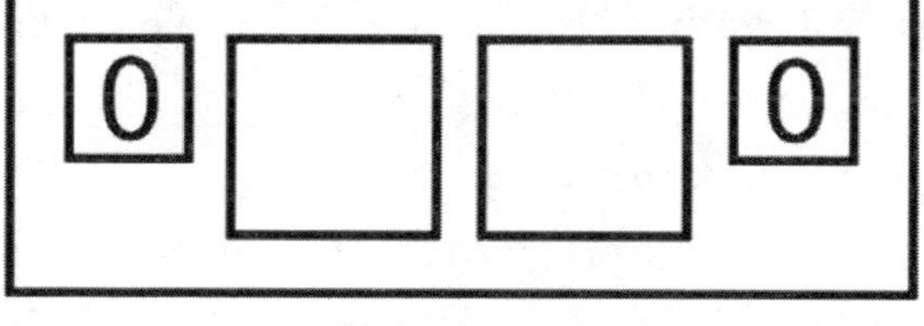

Figure 2: When players arrive
图 2 运动员到场之后

5 If not done earlier, before practice begins, check that the players shown on the score sheet are in the court and are wearing either the correct numbers or have their name displayed, and that their rackets are acceptable. If you leave this until later and there is a wrong player or an illegal racket, time spent practising will have been wasted.

5 如果先前没有完成，在运动员开始练习之前，检查记分单上显示的运动员应出现在比赛区域，号码是否正确或是否佩戴姓名标志，使用的球拍是否合法。如果将这项工作留到后面再做，那么上错了运动员或球拍不合法，先前的练习时间就浪费了。

6 Decide who will have the choice of service and ends by tossing a two coloured disc or a coin in front of both players or pairs, making sure that they know how to call. Do not let the disc or coin fall on the playing surface and, preferably, not on the floor.

6 明确运动员的选择后，当着双方运动员的面旋转两面颜色不同的挑边器或硬币，决定发球权或方位。不要让挑边器或硬币掉落在比赛台面上，更不要掉到地板上。

7 When both players or pairs have made their choices, note on the score card who is the first server and, in doubles, the first receiver. Unless you are certain of the correct way to pronounce the players' names, ask them how they wish their names to be called.

7 当双方运动员做出选择后，在记分单上应注明谁先发球，双打中还要注明谁是第一接发球员。除非你确实知道运动员姓名的正确发音，否则最好问运动员本人怎样被称呼。

8 In an individual event, establish who the designated advisor is for each player or pair. In a team event, check that the number of people on the team bench, including players, coaches and other team officials, does not exceed the permitted number.

8 在单项比赛中，应明确双方运动员或双打运动员的指导者。在团体比赛中，应检查坐在教练员席上的人数（包括运动员、教练员、其他随队官员），确保不超过规定的人数。

9 Give the players a ball that you have taken at random, either from those they have chosen before the match or, if they have not chosen any, from a box of balls of the type specified for the competition.

9 从运动员赛前挑选的球中任意取一个给运动员。如果运动员赛前没有挑球，应从大会指定的一盒比赛用球中随机取一个。

10 Time the practice period and recall players as soon as the permitted time is up. Make sure that they do not receive advice or do anything else to delay the start of play after the practice period has ended.

10 控制练习时间，一旦时间到立即召回运动员。确保运动员在练习时间结束后不能接受指导或做任何延误比赛开始的事情。

11 Before play starts, ensure that towels are placed in a receptacle provided near the umpire or assistant umpire and are not left draped over surrounds. Any other items, such as track suits and bags, should be placed outside the playing area.

11　比赛开始前，应确保擦汗的毛巾放在裁判员或副裁判员附近的容器内而不是悬挂在挡板上。其他任何东西，诸如长袖运动服和背包应放在比赛区域之外。

12　When the players are ready point to and name the first server, call “love-all” or “zero-zero”. In a team match you may use the player’s name or the team name, or both. Set the points score indicators to “0-0” (Figure 3).

12　当运动员准备好后，手指向第一发球员并报出第一发球员的姓名，报“0 比 0”。在团体比赛中，可报球员的姓名或队名或两者都报。将比分显示调至“0∶0”（图 3）。

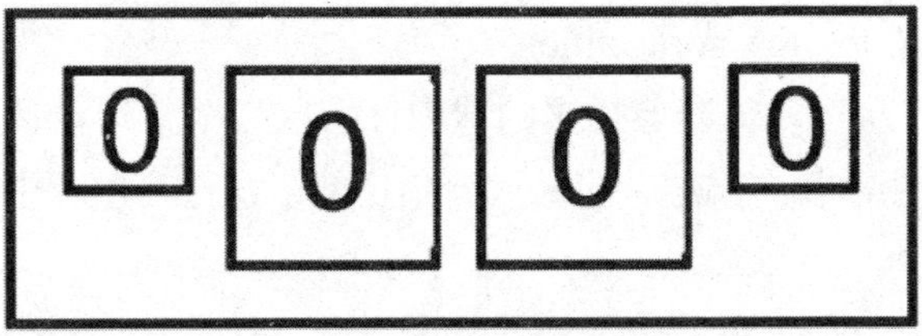

Figure 3: At 0∶0 in 1st game
图 3　第一局 0∶0 时

13　Start the timer as the first player serves and stop and re-start it for substantial breaks in play, such as time spent towelling or retrieving the ball from outside the playing area. Call “time” if play lasts for 10 minutes, unless expedite is already in operation or 18 points in total have been scored.

13　当第一发球员开始发球时，开动计时器。在具体的暂停时段，计时器应及时停止并重新启动，如擦汗和到场外捡球。如果比赛持续了 10 分钟，应报“时间到”，除非已经实行了轮换发球法或双方比分总数都已达到 18 分。

14　After the end of each rally indicated the result by the appropriate hand signal, and as soon as practicable there after by calling the new score, or repeating the last score in the event of a let. If there is to be a change of service, point to the next server. You may also name the next server. Do not change the indicators until the umpire has signaled or called the award of a point (Figure 4).

14　每一个回合结束后，应用适当的手势表示回合的结果，随后尽可能快速报出新比分或回合为重发球时重复原有比分。如果是换发球，应指向下一发球员，也可以报出新的发球员的姓名。在裁判员做手势或宣判比分后再将比分显示器调至新的比分（图 4）。

Figure 4: At 4–6 in 1st game
图 4　第一局 4：6 时

15　Discourage players from wasting time by such means as wandering around the playing area between rallies, persistent bouncing of the ball before serving or prolonged discussion with a doubles partner.

15　不允许运动员用以下方式浪费时间：回合之间在赛区内踱来踱去、发球前长时间拍球或在双打中长时间与同伴商量。

16 During the game, make sure that players are not given advice, either by speech or by signals. On the first occasion warn anyone advising illegally; if the offense is repeat ed, send the advisor away from the playing area for the re mainder of the match or, in a team match, for the remainder of the team match.

16 在一局比赛中，确保运动员不得接受场外语言或手势的指导，任何人第一次非法指导将被警告；如果再次冒犯，指导者将被驱逐出赛场直到该场比赛结束，在团体比赛中，指导者将被驱逐出赛场直到该场团体赛结束。

17 At the end of a game, call the score, announce the winner and the current games score and record the result on the score card. Leave the indicators showing the final points score, without changing the games score (Figure 5). Be alert and look for any misbehaviour immediately following the end of a game.

17 一局比赛结束时，报分，宣布该局的胜方和当时的局分，并记录在记分单上。保留比分显示器最后显示的比分，不要改变局分（图 5)。保持警觉和注意一局比赛结束后立即发生的不良行为。

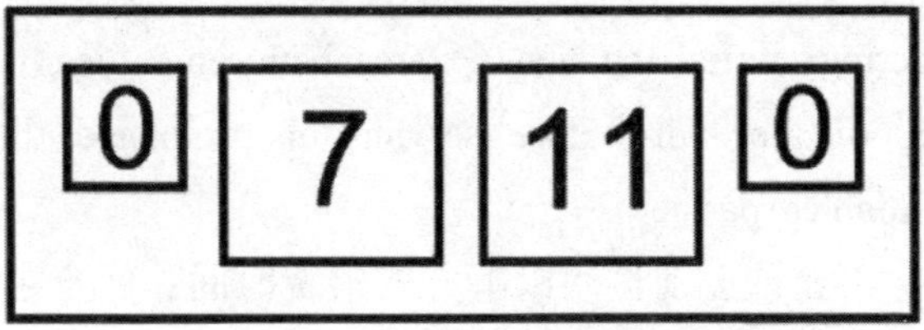

Figure 5: At the end of 1st game
图 5　第一局比赛结束时

18 If necessary, remind players that they must leave their rackets on the table between games unless you give permission for them to be removed. If they are removed, remember that they must be inspected again before the next game. However if the racket is strapped to the hand allow the player to retain it that way.

18 如有必要，提醒运动员在局间必须将球拍留在比赛球台上，除非获得裁判员的许可。如果球拍被带走，记住下一局比赛开始前必须重新检查。如果球拍被绑在运动员的手上，则允许运动员保持球拍捆绑状态。

19 After each game, and during authorised intervals, collect and retain the match ball. Check that surrounds are in their correct positions. Time the interval between games, and other authorised intervals, and recall players as soon as the permitted time is up.

19 每局比赛结束和经许可的间歇时间，收好比赛用球，检查挡板是否摆放整齐。掌控局与局间和其他许可的间歇时间，时间一到立即召回运动员。

20 During intervals, do not wander round the playing area talking to other match officials. Stay in your seat unless you need to move for reasons such as retrieving the ball or adjusting the table, net or surrounds.

20 在间歇时间，不要在比赛区域内走来走去与其他竞赛官员交谈。要坐在裁判椅上，除非需要去捡球或调整球台、球网或挡板。

21 Just before the players return for the next game, set the points score indicators to the blank position and alter the

appropriate games score indicator to reflect the result of the previous game (Figure 6). Remember to change round any yellow or white markers. Set the points indicators to “0 : 0” when the umpire calls that score (Figure 7).

21　在双方运动员返回球台边，准备下局比赛前不久，将比分显示器调至无比分，将局分调至适当的数字以显示前一局的局分（图 6）。记得要交换黄牌或白牌标记。当裁判员报“0比 0”时，将比分显示器调至“0∶0”（图 7）。

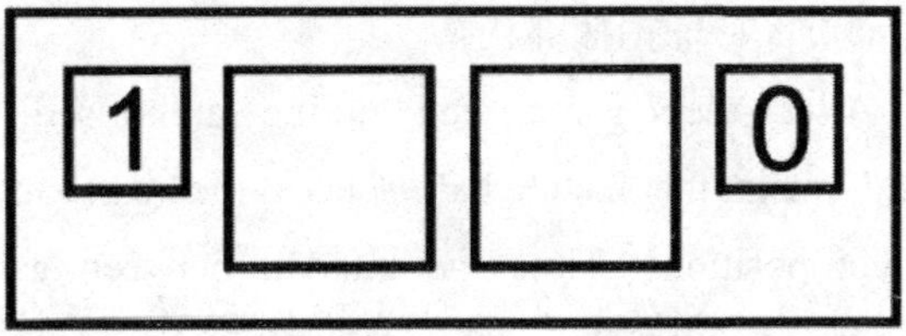

Figure 6: Just before 2nd game
图 6　第 2 局比赛开始前

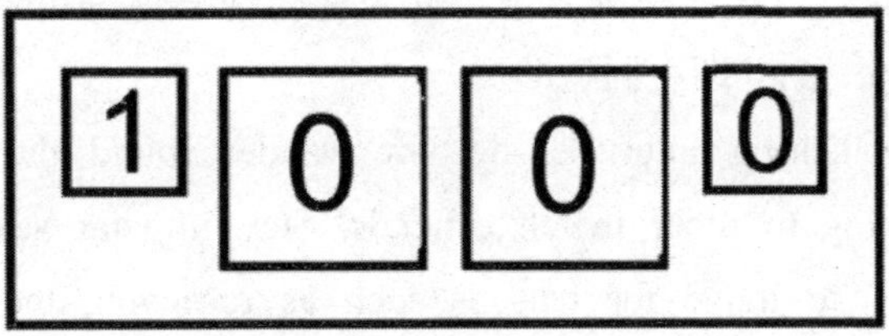

Figure 7: At 0–0 in 2nd game
图 7　第 2 局比赛 0∶0 时

22　At the end of a match, announce the result and, in a team match, the new team match score. Complete the score card and ask the players (in an individual match) or the team captains (in a team match) to sign it, as required. Leave the indicators showing the final points score and the previous games score (Figure 8).

22　一场比赛结束时，宣布比赛结果，在团体比赛中还应宣布当时的场分。完成记分单的填写，如有要求，请运动员（单项比赛中）或队长（团体比赛中）签字。比分显示器上的比分应保留该局的比分和前一局的局分（图8）。

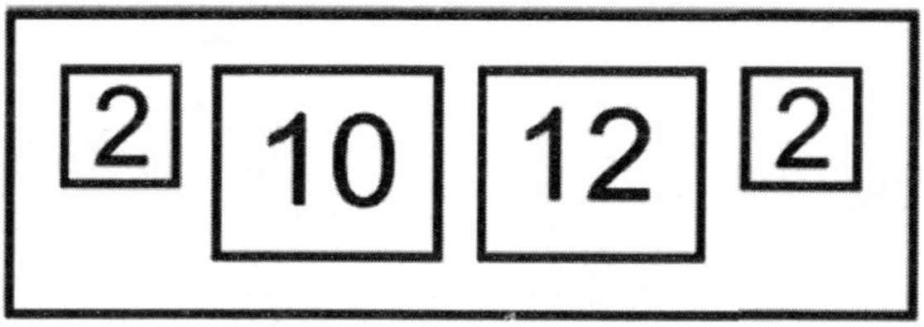

Figure 8: At the end of match
图8　比赛结束时

23　Return the score card promptly to the appropriate officials. Before leaving the playing area, collect the match ball and any spares, as well as any items of clothing, towels or other property that may have been left behind. If necessary collect rackets designated for an after match test. Reset the indicators to the all-blank position (Figure 1).

23　将记分单迅速交给相关的官员。在离开比赛区域前，收好比赛用球及备用球，还有其他东西，如衣服、毛巾或其他遗留在比赛区域的东西。如有必要，收好指定的赛后检测的球拍。将比分显示器调到无任何显示的位置（见图1）。

24　Finally, make sure that you are aware of and are ready to apply any additional procedures or special methods of presentation that have been agreed for the particular competition at which you are officiating; if you are in any doubt, consult the referee.

24　最后，在一些执裁的特定比赛中，应清楚并准备好应用任何已约定的附加程序或特殊表示方法；如有任何疑问，向裁判长请教。

Appendix B——Directives for Match Officials at World Title Competitions and ITTF Sanctioned Events (Revised 2012)

附录 B——世界级比赛和国际乒联批准的赛事中给竞赛官员的指南（2012 年修订）

Definitions

定义

World Title competitions include - but are not limited to - the table tennis competition at the Quadrennial Summer Olympic, World Olympic Qualifications and Youth Olympic Games, the Quadrennial Summer Paralympic Games, the World Team Championships, the World Individual Championships, the World Junior Championships, the World Para Table Tennis Championships, the Men's World Cup, the Women's World Cup, the World Team Cup, and other events so designated by the ITTF Executive Committee.

冠名世界的比赛包括——但不仅限于——每四年一届的夏季奥运会乒乓球比赛、世界奥运会资格赛、青年奥运会、每四年一届的夏季残奥会乒乓球比赛、世界团体锦标赛、世界单项锦标赛、世界青少年锦标赛、世界残疾人乒乓球锦标赛、男子世界杯、女子世界杯、团体世界杯，以及国际乒联执委会指定的其他赛事。

ITTF Sanctioned events include all events so designated

by the ITTF Executive Committee and published on the ITTF calendar from time to time.

国际乒联许可的赛事包括国际乒联执委会指定并不时地公布在国际乒联赛历上的所有赛事。

HOST——HOST Organizing Committee, HOST Association, HOST Governing Body.

主办方——主办方组委会、主办协会、主办国主管机构

URC——The ITTF Umpires and Referees Committee; the Chair of the ITTF Umpires and Referees Committee; any of the designated officials of the ITTF Umpires and Referees Committee.

国际乒联裁委会——国际乒联裁判员和裁判长委员会、国际乒联裁判员和裁判长委员会主席、任何由国际乒联裁判员和裁判长委员会指定的官员。

IR——ITTF certified International Referee.

国际级裁判长——国际乒联认证的国际级裁判长。

IR(C) —— ITTF Certified Referee - individuals who have passed the referee examination, but with insufficient English ability; can officiate as a referee or deputy referee in countries where their language is spoken.

国际级裁判长（国家）——通过裁判长考试但英语能力不足的个人，可以担任母语国家的裁判长或副裁判长。

NR——National Referee (s)——individuals who have successfully completed their Association's internal referee certification program, or the ITTF certified National Referee's Course.

国家级裁判长——顺利完成所属协会内部的裁判长认证课程或国际乒联认证的国家级裁判长课程的个人。

IU——ITTF certified International Umpire.

国际级裁判员——国际乒联认证的国际级裁判员。

NU——National Umpire(s) - individuals who have successfully completed their Association's highest internal umpire certification program, or the ITTF certified National Umpire's Course.

国家级裁判员——顺利完成所属协会内部最高级别的裁判员认证课程，或国际乒联认证的国家级裁判员课程的个人。

Match officials——include referees, umpires, racket testers, evaluators, trainers, referees' coordinator, umpires' coordinator.

比赛官员——包括裁判长、裁判员、球拍检测官、评估师、培训师、裁判长协调官和裁判员协调官。

Number of Referees

Number of Referees = Number of playing halls × 2 + 1.

One more referee will be required for a playing hall with more than 20 tables. If considered warranted 4 referees could be used for one hall of less than 12 tables, especially if the event lasts 4 days or longer.

裁判长数量

裁判长数量 = 场馆数量 × 2 + 1。

超过 20 张比赛球台的场馆需要增加 1 名裁判长。不超过 12 张比赛球台的一个场馆，可以使用 4 名裁判长，特别是比赛持续 4 天或更长时间。

Number of Umpires

World Title Competitions: minimum number of Umpires = Number of tables × 4 + 4.

ITTF Sanctioned Events: minimum number of Umpires = Number of tables × 3,5 + 4.

In events where racket testing is undertaken, the racket control centre must be included as an additional table for the purpose of determining the number of umpires required for the event.

裁判员数量

世界级比赛：裁判员最少数量 = 球台数量 × 4 + 4。

国际乒联批准的比赛：裁判员最少数量 = 球台数量 × 3，5 + 4。

在实行球拍检测的赛事中，应把球拍检测中心视作附加球台考虑，从而决定比赛所需的裁判员数量。

Nomination, Acceptance and Declination of Match Officials

All Referee and Umpire nominations must also be accepted - or declined - by the Association of the nominee.

Age will not be a consideration in the selections of Referees and Umpires.

比赛官员的提名，接受和拒绝

所有裁判长和裁判员的提名也必须得到被提名者所在协会的接受或拒绝。

年龄将不是挑选裁判长和裁判员的考虑因素。

Referees & Deputy Referees

Subject	World Title competitions	ITTF Sanctioned events
Referee	Must be an IR	Must be an IR
Deputy Referee(s)	Must be IRs	At least half must be IRs with no more than one NR
Selection of Referees	By the URC in co-operation with the Host.	By the Host in co-operation with the URC for all IRs. By the Host for one NR
Language	The Referee and all Deputy Referees must be able to communicate in English.	The Referee and all Deputy referees should be able to communicate in English or any language that is common to the players, umpires, referees and Host. It is the responsibility of the Host to make sure that an interpreter is available for the Referee and Deputy Referees if any of them are unable to communicate in English.
Referee mix	At least two-third of the Referees shall be from Associations other than the Host.	At least one-third of the Referees shall be from Associations other than the Host.

(continued table)

Subject	World Title competitions	ITTF Sanctioned events
Referee	The URC will nominate a very competent, qualified and knowledgeable IR with prior experience at major events as the Referee. To ensure neutrality in all aspects of the competition, the IR will not be from the Host. However if the Host has an IR of exceptional quality he or she may also be considered.	The Host will nominate a qualified and experienced IR from the Host. If there are no qualified or experienced IRs from the same continent as the Host, the URC will nominate a qualified and experienced IR from another continent.
Deputy Referees	The URC will nominate additional numbers of qualified and experienced IRs as required, ensuring that either the Referee or one of the Deputy Referees will be from the Host and one from the Host of the next same event - if already designated.	The first Deputy Referee must be an IR or IR(C) from an association other than the Host. The URC will inform the Host about the recommended IR at least 4 months before the event. The second Deputy Referee can be an IR, or IR(C) or NR from the Host or an IRor IR(C) from another association. Subsequent Deputy Referees can be IRs or IR(C)from any continent.

裁判长和副裁判长

事项	世界级比赛	国际乒联批准的比赛
裁判长	必须是国际级裁判长	必须是国际级裁判长
副裁判长	必须是国际级裁判长	至少半数是国际级裁判长，国家级裁判长数量不少过 1 名
裁判长的挑选	由国际乒联裁委会与主办方共同挑选	所有国际级裁判长由国际乒联裁委会与主办方共同挑选 1 名国家级裁判长由主办方挑选
语言	所有裁判长和副裁判长必须能够用英语交流	所有裁判长和副裁判长必须能够用英语或任何一种对运动员、裁判员、裁判长和东道主来说熟悉的语言交流 当裁判长或副裁判长中任何一人不能用英语交流时，主办方有责任确保有一名翻译在场
裁判长队伍的组成	至少应有 2/3 的裁判长来自非主办协会	至少应有 1/3 的裁判长来自非主办协会
裁判长	国际乒联裁委会将任命 1 名拥有重要赛事经验、有能力、有资格和知识渊博的国际级裁判长任裁判长。为了保证竞赛各方面的中立，将不从主办协会挑选国际级裁判长（担任裁判长）。然而，如果主办协会的国际级裁判长品质优异，也可以考虑其任命（担任裁判长）	主办方将从主办协会任命 1 名有资格和有经验的国际级裁判长 如果主办方所在洲没有有资格或有经验的国际级裁判长，国际乒联裁委会将从另一个洲任命 1 名有资格和有经验的国际级裁判长

（续表）

事项	世界级比赛	国际乒联批准的比赛
副裁判长	国际乒联裁委会将按照要求提名有资格和有经验的国际级裁判长担任其余副裁判长，确保裁判长或一名副裁判长来自主办协会和该赛事的下一届主办协会（如果已经指定）	第一副裁判长必须是来自非主办协会的国际级裁判长或国际级裁判长（国家）。国际乒联裁委会将在比赛开始至少 4 个月之前通知主办者所推荐的国际级裁判长。 第二副裁判长可以是来自主办协会的国际级裁判长，或国际级裁判长（国家），或国家级裁判长。或者来自另一个协会的国际级裁判长，或国际级裁判长（国家）。 其余副裁判长可以是来自任何洲的国际级裁判长或国际级裁判长（国家）

Umpires & Assistant umpires

Umpires	Olympic Games: • All umpires and assistant umpires required for the event must be Blue Badge IUs. Youth Olympic Games: • All umpires and assistant umpires required for the event must be IUs or umpires selected based on separate training program of the URC. At least 30% of the umpires must be Blue Badge.	At least one-half of the total number of umpires required for the event must be IUs.

(continued table)

	Paralympic Games: • All umpires and assistant umpires required for the event must be IUs. Umpires selected by the URC must be Blue Badge IUs. Other World Title competitions: • At least 75% of the total number of umpires required for the event must be IUs. • NUs can used for matches at the early stages of the competition (preferably as Assistant Umpires) and may not be used for matches in quarterfinals, semi-finals and finals.	
Foreign IUs	Olympic Games: • There should be only one IU from each Association, with the possibility of up to 1/6 of the total umpires from the Host. Youth Olympic Games: • At least 50% of the umpires shall be from Associations other than the Host. Paralympic Games: • There should be only one IU from each Association with the exception of the Host. Up to 1/3 of the total umpires may be selected by the Host	At least 25% of the umpires shall be from Associations other than the Host, representing at least five associations.

(continued table)

	World Championships, World Junior ChampionshipsWorld Olympic Qualifications and World Para Table Tennis Championships: • At least 50% of the umpires shall be from Associations other than the HOST • The proportion of IU allocation per continent shall be based on ratio of ITTF membership distribution for World Championships and participating team distribution for the World Junior Championships Other World Title competitions: • At least 30% of the umpires shall be from Associations other than the Host, representing at least five associations and including at least three IUs from continents other than the Host. If the total number of umpires on hand does not support such allocation, then a proportional distribution of qualified IUs based on geographical diversity would be suggested by the URC.	

(continued table)

Invitations and Selection of Umpires	Olympic Games: • The URC will directly select all foreign IUs, and the Host will select their umpires. All must be Blue Badge IUs. Youth Olympic Games: • The URC will directly select all foreign IUs, and the Host will select their umpires.	The Host will select the national associations to invite and define the criteria - without specifying any names - which each nominated IU must meet in order to be accepted by the Host.
	Paralympic Games: • The URC will directly select all foreign IUs, as well as up to 6 Host IUs. All must be Blue Badge IUs. The Host will select up to 1/3 of the total umpires.	The Host will invite all NUs and define the criteria that each NU must meet in order to be accepted by the Host.
	World Championships, World Junior Championships, World Olympic Qualifications and World Para Table Tennis Championships: • The URC will invite Associations to nominate any IU meeting a defined set of criteria using each Association's internal selection process. • The URC will select all foreign IUs in cooperation with the Host and define the criteria that the nominated IU must meet in order to be accepted by the URC.	The URC will have the option to nominate up to one-fourth of the total number of foreign umpires in order to provide training and evaluation opportunities for selected IUs to meet global ITTF objectives as well as worldwide geographical diversity.

(continued table)

	• URC nominations will be based on a blend of the levels of IU certification, recent IU activities, personal evaluations and results on written exams, as well as gender and geographic distributions; and for junior events, special considerations may be given to more recently qualified officials. • The Host will nominate all domestic IUs and NUs, and in cooperation with the URC define the criteria that each must meet in order to be accepted by the Host.	The URC will inform the Host of the target associations to be invited at least two months in advance in implementing this option.
Hospitality	All visiting match officials shall be provided with free accommodation, meals and local transport on the same basis and to the same standard as visiting players and with an allowance of US$25 or the equivalent for each day of the competition. The allowance should be paid to the umpires by the second day of the tournament. The Host will pay the lowest cost reasonable economy airfare of the referee and deputy referees.	The Host defines all of the criteria for visiting match officials hospitality, and must clearly include them in the invitation letter to other associations. Any omissions on the standard of hospitality that will be provided are presumed to be at a level equal to - or better than - the level for World Title competitions.

(continued table)

		All visiting match officials shall be provided with an allowance of US$ 25 or the equivalent for each day of the competition. The allowance should be paid to the match officials by the second day of the tournament. The Host will pay the lowest cost reasonable economy airfare of the referee, deputy referees and racket testing coordinator.
Other Match Officials	The URC may appoint a Referees Coordinator and an Umpires Coordinator for the proper governance of the match officials and competition procedures. The URC may invite certified ITTF instructors to conduct training and evaluations for umpires before or during the event, except Olympic and Paralympic Games.	The Host may request from the URC to provide certified ITTF instructors to conduct training and field of play evaluations before or during the event. The Host will provide an office / workplace with computer and internet access for the URC Trainers/Instructors near the field of play.

(continued table)

	The total number of trainers and evaluators will not exceed 1/16 of the total number of umpires working that event - rounded up to the next highest whole number. The Host will provide an office/workplace with computer and internet access for URC/Coordinators near the field of play. The Host will provide hospitality and allowance on the same basis as visiting match officials.	The Host will provide hospitality and allowance on the same basis as visiting match officials.
Field of play procedure	The Host will implement the current ITTF Field of play procedure as defined in the latest version of the ITTF Handbook for Match Officials.	The Host may implement the current ITTF Field of play procedure as defined in the latest version of the ITTF Handbook for Match Officials.
Duty day	Umpires shall be on duty for no more than 8 hours in a day and shall receive at least a 20-minute break every three hours on duty. At World Championships each visiting Umpire shall have 1 free day.	Umpires shall be on duty for no more than 8 hours in a day and shall receive at least a 20-minute break every three hours on duty.

(continued table)

Umpire Uniform	IUs from the same association shall be dressed alike or in the recommended ITTF IU uniform.
Acknowl-edgment	The names and associations of all match officials shall be included in the official programme. In staged matches the names of the umpires for each match shall be announced.
Changing and Storage area for Officials	The Host shall provide a secure changing and storage area near the field of play for all match officials to maintain their personal belonging while on duty.

裁判员和副裁判员

事项	世界级比赛	国际乒联批准的比赛
裁判员	奥运会： 要求所有裁判员和副裁判员必须是蓝牌国际裁判员 青年奥运会： 要求所有裁判员和副裁判员必须是国际级裁判员，或者是通过国际乒联裁委会的单独培训所挑选的裁判员；至少30%是蓝牌 残疾人奥运会： 要求所有裁判员和副裁判员必须是国际级裁判员；国际乒联裁委会所挑选的裁判员必须是蓝牌	要求至少半数的裁判员必须是国际级裁判员

（续表）

事项	世界级比赛	国际乒联批准的比赛
	其他世界级比赛： 要求至少占总数75%的裁判员必须是国际级裁判员； 国家级裁判员可以在比赛的最初阶段使用（最好作为副裁判员），但不能在1/4决赛、半决赛和决赛中使用	
非主办协会的国际级裁判员	奥运会： • 每个协会只能有1名国际级裁判员，最多不超过总数的1/6来自主办协会 青年奥运会： • 至少50%的裁判员来自非主办协会 残疾人奥运会： • 除主办协会外，每个协会只能有1名国际级裁判员；最多不超过总数的1/3由主办协会挑选 世界锦标赛、世界青年锦标赛、奥运会世界资格赛和世界残疾人乒乓球锦标赛： • 至少50%的裁判员应来自非主办协会 每个洲国际级裁判员的分配名额将基于世界锦标赛中国际乒联成员的分配比例和世界青年锦标赛中参赛队的分配比例	至少25%的裁判员应来自非主办协会，至少代表5个协会

（续表）

事项	世界级比赛	国际乒联批准的比赛
	其他世界级的比赛： • 至少 30%的裁判员应来自非主办协会，至少代表 5 个协会并至少包括 3 名国际级裁判员来自非主办方所在洲 如果目前的裁判员总数不满足以上分配名额，则由国际乒联裁委会根据地域多样性按比例推荐有资格的国际级裁判员	
裁判员的邀请和遴选	奥运会： • 国际乒联裁委会直接挑选外籍裁判员，主办方挑选他们自己的裁判员；所有裁判员必须是蓝牌 青年奥运会： • 国际乒联裁委会直接挑选外籍裁判员，主办方挑选他们的裁判员 残疾人奥运会： • 国际乒联裁委会直接挑选外籍裁判员，以及 6 名主办协会的裁判员。所有裁判员必须是蓝牌。主办方将挑选裁判总数 1/3 的裁判员 世界锦标赛、世界青年锦标赛、奥运会世界资格赛和世界残疾人乒乓球锦标赛： • 国际乒联裁委会将邀请各协会使用内部挑选程序，并提名任何一名符合既定标准的国际级裁判员	主办方将挑选协会发出邀请并明确每位被邀请的国际级裁判员（但不提及具体名字）必须满足的标准，以便获得主办方的接受 主办方将邀请所有的国家级裁判员，并明确每位裁判员必须满足的标准，以便获得主办方的接受

（续表）

事项	世界级比赛	国际乒联批准的比赛
裁判员的邀请和遴选	• 国际乒联裁委会将与主办方合作遴选出其他协会的国际级裁判员，并明确被提名的裁判员必须满足的标准，以获得国际乒联裁委会的接受 • 国际乒联裁委会在任命裁判员时，将从国际级裁判员的认证等级、近期执裁情况、个人评价和笔试成绩，以及性别和地域等因素综合考虑。对青年比赛，着重考虑最近获得资格的裁判员 • 主办方将提名所有国内的国际级裁判员和国家级裁判员，并与国际乒联裁委会合作，明确每名裁判员必须满足的标准，以便获得主办方的接受	国际乒联裁委会有权提名外籍裁判员总数 1/4 的裁判员，旨在为所挑选的国际级裁判员提供培训和评价的机会，以实现国际乒联的全球目标和全球地域多样性 在行使挑选权时，国际乒联裁委会将至少提前 2 个月通知主办方所要邀请的协会
接待	应为所有来访的竞赛官员提供免费的食宿和当地交通，接待标准应同运动员。比赛期间，每天提供 25 美元或其他等值货币的补助。补助应在比赛第二天支付 主办方应为裁判长和副裁判长支付花费最低的合理的经济舱机票	主办方应明确所有来访比赛官员的接待标准和补助标准，并写入发给其他协会的邀请函中 应该提供的接待标准中没有提及的部分，将被视为等同于或高于世界级比赛的标准

（续表）

事项	世界级比赛	国际乒联批准的比赛
		比赛期间，应为每位来访的比赛官员提供25美元或其他等值货币的补助。补助应在比赛第二天支付 主办方应为裁判长、副裁判长和球拍检测协调官支付最低合理价格的机票
其他官员	国际乒联裁委会可以任命一名裁判长协调员和一名裁判员协调员，对竞赛官员和比赛程序进行适当管理 在比赛之前或期间，国际乒联裁委会可以邀请一名有资格的国际乒联讲师对裁判员进行培训和评价，奥运会和残疾人奥运会除外 培训和评价讲师的数量不能超过该赛事裁判员总数的1/16 主办方应在比赛区域附近为国际乒联裁委会和协调员提供一个配有电脑和互联网接入的办公室或工作场所 主办方提供接待和补助的标准等同于其他来访的比赛官员	主办方可以请求国际乒联裁委会提供有资格的国际乒联讲师在比赛之前或期间进行培训和临场评价 主办者应在比赛区域附近为国际乒联裁委会的培训员或讲师提供一个配有电脑和互联网接入的办公室或工作场所 主办方提供接待和补助的标准等同于其他来访的比赛官员

（续表）

事项	世界级比赛	国际乒联批准的比赛
比赛区域程序	主办方应执行现行国际乒联比赛区域程序，该程序在最新版的国际乒联竞赛官员手册中明确表述	主办者应执行现行国际乒联比赛区域程序，该程序在最新版的国际乒联竞赛官员手册中明确表述
工作日	裁判员每天工作时间不应超过 8 小时，每 3 小时得到至少 20 分钟的休息 在世界锦标赛中，每位来访的裁判员应有 1 个休息日	裁判员每天工作时间不应超过 8 小时，每 3 小时得到至少 20 分钟的休息
裁判员制服	同一协会的国际级裁判员应着装统一，或穿着国际乒联推荐的国际级裁判员制服	
对裁判工作的肯定	所有竞赛官员的姓名和协会都应写入比赛秩序册 在重要场次的比赛中，应宣布每场比赛裁判员的姓名	
官员的更衣和物品存放区	主办方应在比赛区域附近为所有竞赛官员提供一个更衣和物品存放区，以便他们在工作时存放个人物品	

To achieve ITTF objectives, special consideration should be given to the selection of women for the positions of referee and umpire at all world, Olympic and Paralympic events.

为了实现国际乒联的目标，特别考虑在所有世界、奥运会和残奥会比赛中挑选女性担任裁判长和裁判员。

The URC may have the discretion to waive certain requirements for ITTF sanctioned junior events and the PTT Division may waive certain requirements for PTT event.

国际乒联裁委会有权免除对国际乒联批准的青年赛事的某些要求；国际乒联残疾人乒乓球部可能会免除残疾人乒乓球赛事的某些要求。

The URC, in consultation with the Competition Department, has the discretion to override any of these Directives in exceptional circumstances.

国际乒联裁委会，通过与竞赛部门协商，在特殊情况下有权否决任何以上指南。

Appendix C——Qualifications of Umpires
附录 C——裁判员的资格

The ITTF does not prescribe any standards or test procedures for the qualification of umpires and referees by national associations, however, the ITTF Umpires and Referees Committee (URC) in cooperation with the ITTF Rules Committee provide a degree of commonality and a focal point for the exchange of information and ideas between Associations.

国际乒联没有规定国家级裁判员和国家级裁判长的资格标准或考试程序，然而，国际乒联裁判员和裁判长委员会与规则委员会合作，为了各协会之间能够交换信息和观点而提供一个统一的标准和一个共同关注的重点。

Most associations have 2 to 3 levels of qualifications, with the lowest level being related to a limited geographical area and the highest level having national status. The titles used for the lower grades often reflect smaller geographical area and may include Club Umpire, County Umpire, State Umpire, Provincial Umpire and Regional Umpire. The highest national grade is usually entitled “National Umpire”.

大多数协会将裁判员划分成 2 到 3 个等级，最低的是本地级的，最高的是国家级的。称号等级越低代表地理区域越小，通常为：俱乐部级、乡级、州级、省级、地区级。国内最高级别的裁判员通常称作“国家级裁判员”。

It is up to each association to define and build an appropriate training system for their umpires to prepare them to ward participating at an international level. The training programs should include practical (field of play) as well as theoretical (Laws and Regulations) components.

每个协会负责制定并建立一套合适的裁判员培训体系，为培养本协会的裁判员参与执法国际比赛做好准备。培训课程应包括实践（临场）及理论（规则和规程）部分。

Candidates for the International Umpire (IU) qualifications must be experienced holders of their national association's highest qualification for at least two years. They should also demonstrate a basic level of English comprehension as the base level of communicating with players, coaches and other officials before they are accepted to undergo the IU qualification process.

参加国际级裁判员资格考试的考生必须有两年以上的所属协会国家级裁判员的资历。在参加国际级裁判员资格考试之前，应证明自己具备了一定的英文水平，基本能与运动员、教练员和其他官员交流。

The IU qualification was introduced in 1973, with the objective of providing an internationally accepted "minimum" standard to which umpires of all Associations could become qualified. The IU qualification was not intended as a substitute for a well thought out national education, training and qualifying program.

国际级裁判员资格考试始于 1973 年，其目的是为了提供一个国际上都能接受的且各协会裁判员都有可能通过考试的“最低”标准。国际级裁判员资格考试并不想替代已有健全的国家级裁判员教育、培训和资格课程。

The IU exam typically consists of 50 questions, with four possible options from which to choose the correct answer. The candidate has to select the correct answers within a fixed time period, without using references or help from anyone. Questions are either factual(laws and regulations) or ask what action an umpire should take about a specific situation (field of play). That is why it is critical that umpire experience includes both practical as well as theoretical training.

国际级裁判员考试试卷由 50 道题组成，每道题应从 4 个选项中选出正确的答案。要求考生不借助于参考书或其他人的帮助，在规定的时间内选择正确的答案。问题是实例（规则和规程）或问裁判员在特定的场合（临场）该采取什么行动。这就是为什么要求考生资历必须包括实践和理论培训的重要原因。

Qualifying as an IU demands strong understanding of the laws and regulations, several years of practical “on the table” experience, confidence as an official and a nominal understanding of conversational English as the basis for communication with international players, coaches and other officials.

国际级裁判员应具备较强的对规则和规程的理解能力，有若干年的临场经历，有执法的自信心，有与国外运动员、教练员及其他官员以英文交流的能力。

Once qualified, an IU may have increased opportunity to officiate at competitions outside of their own country. Repetitive and frequent exposure at all levels of international competition is the most important element in building experience and confidence as an active IU.

一旦获得国际级裁判员资格，就有机会去国外执法。作为一名活跃的国际级裁判员，在各种级别的国际性赛事中频频亮相是积累经验和自信的最重要的因素。

In 2002, the ITTF took the first step in building a higher-level qualification for IUs. Through attending the Advance Umpire Training (AUT) course at designated ITTF events, passing an advance level—ITTF supervised—written exam, completing multiple field of play evaluations by different evaluators at various events as well as passing an oral interview, an IU can qualify toward the next level of "Blue" badge certification.

在 2002 年，国际乒联首次开始实施为国际级裁判员设立的更高水平的资格考试。通过参加国际乒联指定赛事中的高级裁判员培训班学习，通过国际乒联监督的高水平的笔试，多次完成在不同赛事中由不同考官主持的临场评估及通过口试，一名国际级裁判员就可以获得更高级别的“蓝牌”资格。

Every year at designated ITTF events, qualified trainers and evaluators will conduct AUT courses as well as field of play evaluations on IUs working those events. The AUT course is designed to impart the ITTF uniform method of performance for all IUs. The evaluation process–with immediate feedback to each umpire –is designed to assist umpires in improving and standardizing their skills toward a uniform high level of performance.

每年，在国际乒联指定的比赛中，合格的培训者和评估者将主持高级裁判员培训班，同时对上场执法的裁判员进行临场评估。高级裁判员培训班的目的是向所有的国际级裁判员传授国际乒联统一的操作程序。评估过程——包括结果及时反馈给每一位裁判员，将有助于提高和规范裁判员的技能朝着统一和高水平的方向发展。

The ITTF umpire evaluation process is not a pass/fail or a grading system, but rather an objective measurement of targeted tasks that must be performed before, during and after each match. Neglecting to perform a designated task is not a failing, but rather an opportunity to improve performance the next time out. Over time with repetitive evaluations and feedback, the quality and standards of umpiring will be reached and can be maintained at a very high level.

国际级裁判员评估过程并不是简单的通过、未通过或评分系统，而是客观评价裁判员在每次赛前、赛中和赛后必须履行的任务的一种手段。在执裁过程中忽视履行某一指定的任务不是失败，而是有机会在下一次比赛中表现得更好。经过几次评估和反馈过程，裁判员的执法质量和标准将会达到并维持在一个非常高的水平。

Umpires attaining - and maintaining their " Blue" badge certification through regular activities and evaluations - will have greater opportunities to be nominated by the ITTF URC to represent their associations at ITTF World Title events.

通过参加常规活动、评估获得并维持“蓝牌”资格的裁判员，将有更多的机会获得国际乒联裁判员和裁判长委员会的提名，代表所属协会参加世界级的比赛。

Excellence, Consistency and Confidence as a match official comes only with experience and an open mind that never stops learning. Consistent performance among all IUs–irrespective of language and cultural differences–is the primary objective of the ITTF umpire qualification process.

作为竞赛官员，优秀、一致性和自信的品质只能来自于经验和永不停止学习的开放心态。不考虑语言和文化差异，国际级裁判员执法的一致性是国际乒联裁判员资格考试的首要目的。

Umpires Progression and Advanced Umpire Training
裁判员发展和高级裁判员培训

Introduction
简介

Since the start of the International Umpires (IU) certification in 1973, the ITTF has qualified more than 5000 IUs. It has set a minimum standard for umpires of all Associations, which have different training methods with no uniform standard of performance.

自 1973 年开始国际级裁判员资格认证以来，国际乒联已经批准了 5000 多名国际级裁判员。它为所有协会的裁判员设定了一个最低的标准，各协会采用不同的培训方法但没有统一的执裁标准。

Since 2002, the Umpires and Referees Committee (URC) of the ITTF has taken an important step towards one of its major objectives: "To raise and level the standard and consistency of umpires from all Associations/Federations".

2002 年，国际乒联裁委会朝着其主要的目标之一"提高和拉平所有协会裁判员的标准和一致性"采取了重要的一步举措。

This has been done by creating two levels of certification for IUs, expressed in the colour of badges, namely the White Badge and the Blue Badge. These badges only exist in name and on paper, IUs will continue to wear the copper-coloured badge issued by the ITTF.

那就是建立了国际级裁判员两种等级的资格认证，以徽章的颜色来表示，即白牌和蓝牌。这些徽章只是称谓和理论上存在，国际级裁判员将继续佩戴由国际乒联颁发的铜色徽章。

White Badge
白牌

All current IUs will be considered as qualified for the White Badge. URC will develop training facilities, and perhaps the exam procedure will be adapted. In the near future there will be additional conditions to maintain the active status, such as secure knowledge of rules.

当前所有的国际级裁判员被认为已获得白牌的资格。国际乒联裁委会将开发培训设施，有可能采用考试程序。在不久的将来，维持现役状态需要附加条件，如牢固的规则知识等。

Blue Badge
蓝牌

Umpires with excellent performance who have the ambition can try to achieve the Blue Badge qualification. This qualification has been and will be an increasing factor in umpire selection.

表现优异，有抱负的裁判员可以尝试获得蓝牌资格，这一资格已成为并逐渐成为裁判选拔的重要因素。

How to qualify for Blue Badge
如何获得蓝牌资格

Requirements:

要求：

- Be an active White Badge umpire for at least 2 years;
- 成为现役白牌裁判至少2年；
- Comply with the URC code of conduct and dress-code;

• 遵守国际乒联行为准则和服装要求；

• Attend the Advanced Umpire Training (AUT) course;

• 参加高级裁判员培训班；

• Pass the written Advanced Rules Examination (ARE);

• 通过高级培训班规则考试；

• Have at least 4 personal evaluations during actual performance with "meets expectations" in each of the defined categories (in a minimum of two competitions from a minimum of three evaluators);

• 获得至少 4 个各项"临场评估合格"（至少在 2 次比赛中从不少于 3 个评估师中得到合格）；

• Pass an oral interview to demonstrate their competency in English to communicate with players and officials during tournaments.

• 通过口试，以示能够在比赛中用英语与运动员和官员沟通。

The examination consists of 60 multiple-choice questions, of which 15 will be only in English, the other 45 will be available translated into 8 other languages: French, German, Spanish, Russian, Chinese, Japanese, Korean and Arabic. This is to ensure that candidates have a sound knowledge in the application of laws and regulations, as well as a reasonable command of English that is required in major ITTF events.

笔试有 60 道多项选择题，其中 15 道是英文，其余 45 道可以译成 8 种语言：法语、德语、西班牙语、俄语、中文、日语、韩语和阿拉伯语。笔试确保候选人能熟练地运用规则和规程，同时适当地掌握国际乒联主要赛事要求的英文。

Additional requirements

其他条件：

• The umpire must have participated as an IU in at least 2 international events;

• 作为国际级裁判员至少参加2次国际比赛；

• The 4 "meets expectations" should be obtained in a minimum of two competitions from a minimum of three different evaluators;

• 至少在2次比赛中从不少于3个不同的评估师中得到4个“临场评估合格”；

• After obtaining the first "meets expectations" the remaining 3 should be obtained within 7 attempts;

• 获得第一个“临场评估合格”后，剩余的3个合格必须在不超过7次临场评估中获得；

• No evaluations can be from an evaluator from that umpire's own association;

• 同一协会的评估师不参与临场评估；

• After obtaining the 4th "meets expectations" the candidate will have a maximum of 12 months to take the English interview;

• 获得4个“临场评估合格”后，候选人在最长12个月内参加英文面试；

• If the candidate fails the English interview they will have a maximum of 2 years from their first interview to re-take it;

• 如果候选人未通过英文面试，从第一次面试算起到再次参加，最长时间为2年；

• The Blue Badge process must be completed in 5 years or less from the time of passing the Advanced Rules Examination;

• 从通过高级培训班规则考试开始，必须在 5 年或 5 年内完成蓝牌过程；

• Candidates not taking the interview in time or not completing the Blue Badge process in 5 years, revert to the White Badge status and must restart through the complete Blue Badge procedure;

• 候选人没有及时参加面试，或未能在 5 年内完成蓝牌过程，将回到白牌地位，必须重新完成蓝牌过程；

• For evaluations performed in 2006 or later, a "meets expectation" would only be counted after passing the written examination;

• 对 2006 年及以后的临场评估，只有通过笔试，"临场评估合格"方能有效；

• Evaluations only count if the umpire is part of the regular umpires squad, performing daily duties, but not tournament officials who officiate only for the sake of evaluation;

• 裁判员是临场裁判员队伍的一员，每日上场执裁，评估才能有效；比赛官员仅仅为了被评估而上场执裁，则评估无效；

• Any "meets expectation" evaluations are only considered as "conditional meets", which will only be confirmed after continuous observation further evaluation throughout the tournament. Any inconsistent or poor performance would result in deletion of such positive result, and the trainer will notify the umpire;

• 任何获得的“临场评估合格”只能被认为是“有条件的合格”，只有在整个赛事中不停地被观察和进一步评估，“临场评估合格”最后才会被确认；任何临场不一致或表现差将导致“临场评估合格”被删除，培训师将通知该裁判员；

• After having obtained the first “meets expectation” getting a “does not meet” (not a “near”) will cancel a “meets expectation”;

• 在获得一个“临场评估合格”后，紧接着得到一个“临场评估不合格”（不是“接近合格”），前一个合格将被抵消；

• If a Blue-Badge candidate is not present at the “Referee’s briefing” he or she will not be evaluated during the respective event, unless the absence was for an acceptable reason, at the discretion of the evaluator.

• 如果蓝牌候选人未参加裁判长赛前短会，他（她）在各自的比赛中将不会被评估，除非缺席的理由可以被评估师接受。

How to maintain the Blue Badge status
如何维持蓝牌地位

Requirements:

要求：

• In a period of 3 calendar years at least 3 personal evaluations during actual performance with “meets expectations” in each of the defined categories;

• 3 年内获得至少 3 个各项“临场评估合格”；

• Meet the current re-certification process of White Badge umpires, as soon as re-certification is in place;

• 一旦资格重新认证开始，符合现行白牌裁判的资格重新开始认证过程；

• The 3 “meets expectations” should be obtained in a minimum of two competitions from a minimum of two different evaluators;

• 至少在2次比赛中从不少于2个不同的评估师中得到3个“临场评估合格”；

• No evaluation can be from an evaluator from that umpire's own association;

• 来自同一协会的评估师不参与临场评估；

• After passing the oral interview any further “meets” will count for the following period of 3 years for maintaining the blue-badge qualification, but “meets” between the 4th “meets” and the oral interview shall not be reckoned;

• 通过口试以后获得的“临场评估合格”在维持蓝牌资格的接下来3年内有效，但在第4个“临场评估合格”与口试之间获得的“临场评估合格”无效；

• Blue Badge umpires not meeting these requirements by December 31 of any year, would be qualified as White Badge umpires for the following year;

• 蓝牌裁判在任何一年的12月31日未达到以上要求，将在下一年成为白牌裁判。

Former Blue Badge umpires who lose their status may regain their Blue Badge status by meeting the requirement of 4 “meets expectations” in 2 successive calendar years.

失去蓝牌资格的前蓝牌裁判员可在连续2年之内获得4个“临场评估合格”而重新复位。

Advanced Umpires Training Courses
高级裁判员培训课程

The AUT course is normally scheduled one day before the start of several ITTF sanctioned events. White Badge umpires officiating in these events are invited to attend the training. The URC will announce the schedule of the organised AUT courses on the website; umpires who are not officiating in the event are also welcome to attend the course.

高级裁判员培训课程通常安排在国际乒联许可的一些赛事开赛的前一天。执裁这些赛事的白牌裁判员被邀请参加培训。国际乒联裁委会将在网站上宣布高级裁判员培训课程的安排，同时欢迎不执裁赛事的裁判员也参加培训课程。

The training is based on the concept: “I hear and I forget, I see and I remember, I do and I understand”. There is a high degree of active participation.

培训是建立在“听到的我会忘记，看到的我会记住，做到的我会理解”这一理念上，这是高度的积极参与。

Global summary of subjects:

总体课程概要：

- Introduction activities;
- 相互介绍；
- Code of conduct & dress-code;
- 行为准则和服装；
- Standards for service & behaviour;
- 发球标准和行为准则；

- Hand signals & field of play procedures;
- 手势和临场操作程序；
- Evaluations;
- 评估；
- Knotty problems;
- 疑难问题；
- Written exam.
- 笔试。

The training does not cover the material asked in the Advanced Rules Exam. Participants must have a very strong knowledge of rules and must be up to date on recent rule changes. The examination and oral interview may not be re-taken less than 12 months since the last attempt, and not more than twice within a five-year period.

培训内容并不全部覆盖高级培训班规则考试中提出的问题，参加者必须牢固掌握规则并拥有规则变化的最新信息。笔试和口试如未通过，1 年以后才能再次参加，并且 5 年内不得超过 2 次。

Attending the AUT and passing the ARE are prerequisites for those who want to become Blue Badge umpires. The ARE can be taken before or after attending the AUT. The ARE will be a supervised exam with the supervisor being ap pointed by URC.

想成为蓝牌裁判必须参加高级裁判员培训课程和通过高级培训班规则考试。高级培训班规则考试可以在参加高级裁判员培训课程前或课程后进行。国际乒联裁委会将指派考官监督高级培训班规则考试。

The Trainers

培训师

The trainers for AUT courses are experienced International Umpires / Referees who are nominated by their respective Continental Federations or identified by the URC during the course. All trainers are specially trained and updated regularly on requirements of the Blue Badge Programme, with an aim to maintain consistent application of laws and regulations, as well as a standard presentation at major ITTF events.

高级裁判员培训班的培训师由经验丰富的国际级裁判员/裁判长担任，他们由各自的洲联合会提名或由国际乒联裁委会确定。所有培训师经过特别培训并定期掌握蓝牌课程的最新要求，旨在保持规则和规程运用的一致性，以及国际乒联重大赛事的统一展示。

Costs for Participants

参加者费用

A course fee will be charged, which will include attending the course, and the field of play evaluations, and the evaluations thereafter in subsequent tournaments. However, if a candidate fails in the written examination, there will be no more field of play evaluations conducted until he or she takes the examination again. A separate fee will be charged for the ARE.

将收取课程费用，包括参加培训课程、临场评估以及后续比赛的评估费用。然而，如果候选人未能通过笔试，他（她）就不会被评估，直至下次通过笔试。这种情况将另外收取笔试费用。

Participants are required to pay for the extra personal costs (e.g. hotel and food) when arriving one day earlier.

提前一天抵达的参加者需要支付额外的个人费用（如住宿和餐饮费）。

Costs for Organisers

主办方费用

For URC selected events, ITTF will be responsible for the following costs:

对于国际乒联裁委会选定的赛事，国际乒联将负责以下费用：

- Travelling expenses and training fee for the appointed trainers;
- 指定培训师的交通费和培训费；
- Course and examination materials.
- 培训班和笔试资料。

The Organisers are responsible for the following:

主办方负责以下费用：

- Hospitality (accommodation + meals + local travelling + daily allowance) for the trainers;
- 培训师的接待（住宿 + 餐饮 + 当地交通费用 + 每日津贴）；

- Airport transfer and local transportation for the trainers;
- 培训师的机场接送和当地交通；
- Training facilities - classroom, equipment such as computer, projector, screen, white board, flip charts, copying services, etc;
- 培训设施，包括教室，计算机、投影仪、屏幕、白板、活动挂图、复印服务等设备；
- Refreshments during breaks would be appreciated.

休息时间如提供茶点，将非常感谢。

To qualify for the ITTF expenses, a minimum of 12 and maximum 25 participants from at least three different Associations are required. Two trainers will be assigned to the AUT course and evaluations, and additional trainers may be required for more than 25 participants.

国际乒联支付费用的条件是培训班的人数最少 12 人，最多 25 人，并且来自 3 个不同的协会。2 名评估师将被指派主持课程和评估，超过 25 人需要更多的评估师。

Other Special Considerations

其他特别考虑

The URC may also send trainers to specific events upon request of the Organisers, who agree to cover all related costs of the course, including transportation and honorarium for trainers.

如果主办方同意支付培训班所有的相关费用，包括培训师的交通费和酬金，国际乒联裁委会将根据主办方的请求，指派培训师到指定赛事。

Priority is also given to regions and special groups (such as women in sport), where the Blue Badge Programme is less developed. Requirements for the AUT course may also be relaxed (e.g. fewer participants / Associations) at the discretion of the URC.

优先考虑蓝牌项目不发达的地区和特殊群体（如女子运动），国际乒联裁委会有权放宽对高级裁判员培训班的要求（如参加人数 / 协会较少）。

Consideration will also be given to sending evaluators to events, where no AUT course is held, where the organiser agrees to cover the costs of the evaluators.

如果不举办高级裁判员培训班，主办方同意支付评估师的相关费用，国际乒联裁委会也可以考虑指派评估师到相应赛事。

Contact

Organisers wishing to organise an AUT course, or to have trainers/evaluators at their events, please contact the Chair of the URC.

联系

主办方有意愿组织高级裁判员培训班，或在其赛事中邀请培训师 / 评估师，请联系国际乒联裁委会主席。

Appendix D——Match Officials Code of Conduct

附录 D——竞赛官员行为准则

1 Match officials, especially while in uniform, are ambassadors of the sport, of the ITTF and of their Associations. At an international competition they are the guests of the Host Association and must respect its traditions and social customs. The following guidelines, which are not exhaustive, are intended as an aide-memoire on the aspects of conduct to which special attention should be given.

1 比赛官员，尤其是在穿着制服的时候，是乒乓球运动、国际乒联和他们所在协会的代表。在国际比赛中，他们是主办协会的客人，必须遵守当地的传统习惯和社会习俗。以下的准则，不是完全详尽的，旨在作为行为方面应特别注意的事项的辅助备忘录。

2 MATCH OFFICIALS SHOULD

2 比赛官员应该做到

2.1 Study and make sure they understand all the relevant rules, duties and procedures for the competition at which they are officiating;

2.1 对将要执法比赛的所有相关规则、职责和程序进行研究并确保理解；

2.2 Be in good physical condition, with normal or corrected vision and normal hearing;

2.2 保持良好的身体状况，视力或矫正的视力和听力正常；

2.3 Be in appropriate uniform and maintain their appearance and personal hygiene;

2.3 穿着合适的制服，保持良好的形象和个人卫生；

2.4 Be prompt for all assignments;

2.4 能迅速执行所有的任务；

2.5 Maintain strict impartiality and avoid any relationship with players or coaches that might cast doubt on that impartiality;

2.5 严格保持执法的公平性，避免任何与运动员和教练员有关的、可能对执法公正性产生怀疑的联系；

2.6 Refer all issues not related to their duties to the Referee or other appropriate tournament official;

2.6 遇到与自己执法职责无关的事宜，交由裁判长或其他相关竞赛官员处理；

2.7 Wherever practical, avoid unaccompanied and unobserved one-on-one activity (when in a supervisory capacity or where a power imbalance may exist) particularly with people under the age of 18 years;

2.7 只要条件允许，避免没有同伴和监督的、单独的一对一活动（当有监管能力或权力不平衡的情况时），特别是与18岁以下的人士；

2.8 Ensure their decisions and actions contribute to a safe environment;

2.8 保证他们的决定和行为有利于营造安全的环境；

2.9 Ensure their decisions and actions contribute to a harassment free environment;

2.9 保证他们的决定和行为有助于营造没有骚扰的环境；

2.10 At all times conduct themselves in a professional and ethical manner, respecting the authority and interests of the referee, the organisers, other tournament officials, players and the public.

2.10 始终以职业的和道德的方式为人处世，尊重裁判长、主办方、其他比赛官员、运动员和公众的权利和利益。

3 MATCH OFFICIALS SHOULD NOT

3 比赛官员不应该做的

3.1 Discuss tournament incidents or other issues related to their duties with players, spectators or media, but should refer any such matters to the referee and the tournament committee;

3.1 不与运动员、观众、媒体谈论比赛事件或其他与其职责有关的问题，而任何此类问题应交由裁判长和竞赛委员会处理；

3.2 Accept personal gifts from players, coaches and teams. Gifts provided by a host organization to all officials can be accepted;

3.2 不接受教练员、运动员和参赛队的个人礼物，由主办单位提供给所有官员的礼物可以接受；

3.3 Consume alcoholic beverages or take drugs or medications that will inhibit performance before their match on the day they are to officiate;

3.3 不在将要执裁的当天，喝含酒精的饮料或服用抑制机体性能的药物；

3.4 Publicly criticize other officials or otherwise bring the sport into disrepute, including use of social media;

3.4 不公开批评其他官员或诋毁本项运动声誉，包括利用社会传媒；

3.5 Tolerate harmful or abusive behaviours but report them to the Chair of the URC where the issue is not resolved to the satisfaction of the parties concerned;

3.5 不容忍有害和不端的行为；相反，如果事件未得到相关各方满意的解决，应向国际乒联裁委会主席汇报；

3.6 As with the high standard of professionalism and conduct required of players, ITTF requires a high standard of professionalism and conduct from its officials as well as all officials participating in ITTF sanctioned and recognized events. ITTF officials not observing the stated guidelines may be subject to a formal disciplinary process.

3.6 随着对运动员职业作风和品行的高标准要求，国际乒联对所有参加其批准和认可赛事的官员，以及其他官员的职业作风和品行也提出了高标准的要求。不遵守上述准则的国际乒联竞赛官员，将受到正式的纪律处罚。

Please refer to the ITTF Handbook for the policies adopted in relation to Anti-Harassment and Illegal Betting and Corruption. The URC reserves the right to take action if an official deviates from this code of conduct.

关于反骚扰、非法赌博和腐败的问题，请查看国际乒联手册的相关政策。对任何有违法行为的竞赛官员，国际乒联裁委会保留采取行动的权力。

Appendix E——Recommended Hand Signals and Calls

附录 E——推荐的手势和宣告

1. Next server
图 1　下一发球方

2. Let
图 2　重发球

3. Point
图 3　得分

When making hand signals ensure that they are clearly separated. For example do not indicate a point with one arm and at the same time indicate the next server with the other arm.

手势应明显分开。例如，不应在一只手臂做得分手势时，另一只手臂做下一发球方手势。

	A	B	C	D	E
1	SITUATION	UMPIRE´S SIGNAL	UMPIRE´S CALL	AU´S SIGNAL	AU´S CALL
2	Start of game	Point with open hand to first server [1]	"X to serve, 0-0" (or other agreed announcement)	None	None
3	Change of service	Point with open hand to next server [1]	None	None	None
4	Resumption of play after authorised interval	Point with open hand to next server [1]	Repeat score	None	None
5	Point	Raise the arm nearer the winner(s) of the point so that the upper arm is horizontal and the forearm vertical, with the closed hand upward [3]	New score	None	None

(continued table)

	A	B	C	D	E
	SITUATION	UMPIRE´S SIGNAL	UMPIRE´S CALL	AU´S SIGNAL	AU´S CALL
6	Net-cord service	As soon as the ball touches the correct court raise arm above head [2], point to net if necessary	"Let" and repeat previous score	As soon as the ball touches the correct court raise arm above head [2], point to net if necessary	None*
7	Illegal service	Raise the arm nearer the receiver so that the upper arm is horizontal and the forearm vertical, with the closed hand upward [3]	"Fault" and new score	Raise arm above head [2]	"Fault" and advise umpire if necessary who will call new score
8	In doubles service, ball bounces on wrong half-court	Indicate point for receiver [3], point to centreline if necessary.	"Fault" and new score	None	None
9	Faulty service (e.g. ball misses table)	Indicate point for receiver [3]	New score	None	None

(continued table)

	A	B	C	D	E
	SITUATION	UMPIRE´S SIGNAL	UMPIRE´S CALL	AU´S SIGNAL	AU´S CALL
10 a	Service of doubtful legality where decided by the umpire (1st occasion in a match)	Raise arm above head [2]	"Let", warn server, and repeat previous score	None	None
10 b	Service of doubtful legality where decided by the assistant umpire (1st occasion in a match)	Raise arm above head [2]	"Let", and repeat previous score	Raise arm above head [2]	"Stop", warn server and advise umpire, who will call "Let"
11 a	Service of doubtful legality where decided by the umpire (further occasion by same player or pair)	Indicate point for receiver [3]	"Fault" and new score	None	None
11 b	Service of doubtful legality where decided by the assistant umpire (further occasion by same player or pair)	Indicate point for receiver [3]	New score	Raise arm above head [2]	"Fault", if necessary advise umpire, who will call new score

(continued table)

	A	B	C	D	E
	SITUATION	UMPIRE´S SIGNAL	UMPIRE´S CALL	AU´S SIGNAL	AU´S CALL
12	Interruption of play (e.g. ball coming into playing area)	Raise arm above head [2]	"Let" and repeat previous score	Raise arm above head [2]	"Stop"
13	Error in order of serving, receiving or ends discovered during a rally	Raise arm above head [2]	"Let", correct order and repeat previous score	None	None
14	Advice given during play, first occurrence	Raise arm above head[2] holding up a yellow card towards offender, without leaving chair	"Let", if ball is in play, warn adviser and repeat previous score	Raise arm above head [2]	"Stop" and inform umpire
15	Advice given during play, subsequent occurrence	Raise arm above head [2] holding up a red card towards offender, without leaving chair	"Let", if ball is in play, send adviser away from the playing area, and repeat previous score	Raise arm above head [2]	"Stop" and inform umpire

(continued table)

	A	B	C	D	E
	SITUATION	UMPIRE´S SIGNAL	UMPIRE´S CALL	AU´S SIGNAL	AU´S CALL
16	Ball obstructed by player	Indicate point for the winner (s) of the point [3]	New score	Raise arm above head [2]	“Stop” and advise umpire
17	Any other situation which does not automatically stop play	Raise arm above head [2]	“Stop” and new score, plus any additional call necessary under 18.4	None	None
18	Edge ball at side nearest to AU ending the rally	Indicate point for the winner (s) of the point [3]	New score	Point to place of contact if necessary	“Edge"
19	Edge ball at any other side ending the rally	Indicate point for the winner (s) of the point [3] Point to place of contact if necessary	New score	None	None
20	Ball hits side of table top nearest to AU ending the rally	Indicate point for the winner (s) of the point [3]	New score	Raise arm above head [2]	“Side"

(continued table)

	A	B	C	D	E
	SITUATION	UMPIRE´S SIGNAL	UMPIRE´S CALL	AU´S SIGNAL	AU´S CALL
21 a	Time reached for end of practice or between games (if assistant umpire is timekeeper)	None	None	Raise arm above head [2]	"Time"
21 b	Time reached for end of practice or between games (if umpire is timekeeper)	Raise arm above head [2]	"Time"	None	None
22	Time limit (if assistant umpire is timekeeper)	Raise arm above head [2], after AU's signal and call	"Let" if necessary, announce that expedite will apply and repeat previous score	Raise arm above head [2]	"Time"
23	Time limit (if umpire is timekeeper)	Raise arm above head [2]	"Time", announce that expedite will apply and repeat previous score	None	None

(continued table)

	A	B	C	D	E
	SITUA–TION	UMPIRE´S SIGNAL	UM–PIRE´SCALL	AU´S SIGNAL	AU´S CALL
24	Request for time-out	Raise arm above head [2] holding up white card to the side of the player or pair requesting the time-out until the AU has placed a special signboard on the table	"Time-out"	Place a special signboard (or white marker) on court of requesting player or pair. Stand next to the AU table until it is timc to remove signboard (or white marker)	None
25	Request for time-out(if no assistant umpire)	Raise arm above head [2] holding up white card to the side of the player or pair requesting the time-out	"Time-out"		
26	End of time-out (if assistant umpire is timekeep-er)	When players return, point with open hand to next server [1]	Repeat previ-ous score	Remove special signboard (or white marker) from table and place white marker by score indicator	Raise arm above head [2] and call "Time" if players have not returned

(continued table)

	A	B	C	D	E
	SITUATION	UMPIRE´S SIGNAL	UMPIRE´S CALL	AU´S SIGNAL	AU´S CALL
27	End of time-out (if umpire is timekeeper)	When players return, point with open hand to next server [1]	Raise arm above head [2] and call "Time" if players have not returned; repeat previous score	Remove special signboard (or white marker) from table and place white marker by score indicator	None
28	Bad behaviour (1st occasion)	Hold up yellow card towards offender, without leaving chair	"Let" if ball is in play, warn offender and repeat previous score	Raise arm above head [2] Place yellow marker by score indicator	"Stop" and inform umpire
29	Bad behaviour (2nd and 3rd occasions)	Hold up yellow and red card towards offender, without leaving chair, indicate point for the winner(s) of the point [3]	"Let", if ball is in play, new score after awarding penalty point (s)	Raise arm above head [2] Place yellow/red markers by score indicator if space allows	"Stop" and inform umpire

(continued table)

	A	B	C	D	E
	SITUATION	UMPIRE´S SIGNAL	UMPIRE´S CALL	AU´S SIGNAL	AU´S CALL
30	End of game	Point with open hand to winner [1]	Game score and agreed post-game announcement	None	None
31	End of match	Point with open hand to winner [1]	Match score and agreed post-match announcement	None	None

	A	B	C	D	E
1	**情景**	**裁判员的手势**	**裁判员的宣告**	**副裁判员的手势**	**副裁判员的宣告**
2	一局比赛开始	手掌张开指向第一发球员[1]（角注的“1、2、3”指前图的1、2、3）	“X 发球，0 比 0”（或其他商议好的宣告）	无	无
3	换发球	手掌张开指向下一发球员[1]	无	无	无
4	经许可的间歇后继续比赛	手掌张开指向下一发球员[1]	重复比分	无	无
5	得分	将靠近得分方的手臂举起，使上臂水平，前臂垂直，手握拳向上[3]	新比分	无	无

（续表）

	A	B	C	D	E
	情景	裁判员的手势	裁判员的宣告	副裁判员的手势	副裁判员的宣告
6	发球擦网	一旦球触及规定的台区，立即将手臂高举过头[2]，如有必要，手指向网	“重发球”并重复原有比分	一旦球触及规定的台区，立即将手臂高举过头[2]，如有必要，手指向网	无 *
7	发球违例	将靠近得分方的手臂举起，使上臂水平，前臂垂直，手握拳向上[3]	“违例”并报新比分	将手臂高举过头[2]	“违例”，如有必要告知裁判员，裁判员将报新比分
8	双打发球，球落在错误的半区	接发球方得分[3]，如有必要，手指向中线	“违例”并报新比分	无	无
9	发球违例（如发球出界）	接发球方得分[3]	新比分	无	无
10a	裁判员对发球有怀疑（一场比赛中第一次出现）	将手臂高举过头[2]	“重发球”，警告发球员，并重复原有比分	无	无

（续表）

	A	B	C	D	E
	情景	裁判员的手势	裁判员的宣告	副裁判员的手势	副裁判员的宣告
10 b	副裁判员对发球有怀疑（一场比赛中第一次出现）	将手臂高举过头[2]	“重发球”并重复原有比分	将手臂高举过头[2]	“停”，警告发球员并告知裁判员，裁判员将报“重发球”
11 a	裁判员对发球有怀疑（同一名/对选手第二次出现）	接发球方得分[3]	“违例”并报新比分	无	无
11 b	副裁判员对发球有怀疑（同一名/对选手第二次出现）	接发球方得分[3]	新比分	将手臂高举过头[2]	“违例”，如有必要告知裁判员，裁判员将报新比分
12	比赛中断（如外界球进入比赛区域）	将手臂高举过头[2]	“重发球”并重复原有比分	将手臂高举过头[2]	“停”
13	回合中发现发球、接发球或方位错误	将手臂高举过头[2]	“重发球”，纠正次序并重复原有比分	无	无

（续表）

	A	B	C	D	E
	情景	裁判员的手势	裁判员的宣告	副裁判员的手势	副裁判员的宣告
14	赛中非法指导，第一次出现	将手臂高举过头[2]，向冒犯者出示黄牌，不要离开裁判椅	如果球仍处于比赛状态，报“重发球”，警告指导者，并重复原有比分	将手臂高举过头[2]	“停”，并告知裁判员
15	赛中非法指导，第二次出现	将手臂高举过头[2]，向冒犯者出示红牌，不要离开裁判椅	如果球仍处于比赛状态，报“重发球”，将指导者驱逐出比赛区域，并重复原有比分	将手臂高举过头[2]	“停”，并告知裁判员
16	运动员阻挡	胜方得分[3]	新比分	将手臂高举过头[2]	“停”，并告知裁判员
17	任何其他不能自动终止的回合的情况	将手臂高举过头[2]	“停”并报新比分，如有必要，可按照18.4加上额外的宣告	无	无
18	靠近副裁判员一侧的擦边球，回合结束	胜方得分[3]	新比分	如有必要，手指向球触及的球台处	“擦边”
19	其他处的擦边球，回合结束	胜方得分[3]，如有必要，手指向球触及的球台处	新比分	无	无

（续表）

	A	B	C	D	E
	情景	裁判员的手势	裁判员的宣告	副裁判员的手势	副裁判员的宣告
20	球触及靠近副裁判员一侧球台的侧面，回合结束	胜方得分[3]	新比分	将手臂高举过头[2]	“侧面”
21a	练习时间结束或局间休息结束（如果副裁判员计时）	无	无	如果计时，将手臂高举过头[2]	“时间到”
21b	练习时间结束或局间休息结束（如果裁判员计时）	将手臂高举过头[2]	“时间到”	无	无
22	比赛时限到（如果副裁判员计时）	等副裁判员做完手势和宣告后，将手臂高举过头[2]	“重发球”，如有必要，宣布实行轮换发球法，并重复原有比分	将手臂高举过头[2]	“时间到”
23	比赛时限到（如果裁判员计时）	将手臂高举过头[2]	“时间到”，宣布实行轮换发球法，并重复原有比分	无	无

（续表）

	A	B	C	D	E
	情景	裁判员的手势	裁判员的宣告	副裁判员的手势	副裁判员的宣告
24	请求暂停	将手臂高举过头[2]，向要求暂停一方高举白牌，直至副裁判员将特别标志物放在球台上	暂停	将特别的标志物（或白色标识）放在要求暂停一方的台区上。站在裁判台一侧直至时间到时拿走特别标志物（或白色标识）	无
25	请求暂停（如果没有副裁判员）	将手臂高举过头[2]，向要求暂停一方高举白牌	暂停		
26	暂停时间结束（如果副裁判员计时）	当运动员返回时，手掌张开指向下一发球员[1]	重复原有比分	从球台上拿走特别标志物（或白色标识），将白色标识放在翻分器旁	将手臂高举过头[2]，如果运动员没有返回，报“时间到”
27	暂停时间结束（如果裁判员计时）	当运动员返回时，手掌张开指向下一发球员[1]	将手臂高举过头[2]，如果运动员没有返回，报“时间到”，重复原有比分	从球台上拿走特别标志物（或白色标识），将白色标识放在翻分器旁	无

（续表）

	A	B	C	D	E
	情景	裁判员的手势	裁判员的宣告	副裁判员的手势	副裁判员的宣告
28	不良行为(第一次出现)	向冒犯者出示黄牌，不要离开裁判椅	如果球仍处于比赛状态，报"重发球"，警告冒犯者，并重复原有比分	将手臂高举过头[2]，将黄色标识放在翻分器旁	"停"，并告知裁判员
29	不良行为(第二次和第三次出现)	向冒犯者出示红黄牌，不要离开裁判椅；对方得分	如果球仍处于比赛状态，报"重发球"，罚分后报新比分	将手臂高举过头[2]，将黄色和红色标识放在翻分器旁（如果空间足够）	"停"，并告知裁判员
30	一局比赛结束	张开手掌指向获胜方[1]	局分，商议好的局后宣告	无	无
31	一场比赛结束	张开手掌指向获胜方[1]	场分，商议好的赛后宣告	无	无

When the ball touches the net during service, the umpire should wait until the ball touches the correct court and make the appropriate call, rather than introduce an additional signal before the rally is over that may interfere with play.

Superscript numbers in the table refer to the Hand Signals diagrams.

发球过程中，当球触网时，裁判员应等到球触及正确的台区后再做相应的宣告，而不要在回合结束前做多余的手势，这会干扰比赛。

* if the service is a let and the umpire does not stop play then the assistant umpire should call “Stop”.

* 如应重发球而裁判员并未中止比赛，副裁判员应喊“停”。

表中的上标数字代表相应的手势简图编号。

Appendix F——Field of play Procedures
附录 F——临场操作程序

INTRODUCTION
介绍

Everything that is visible and can occur within the view of spectators and media (reporters, television, and photographers) is considered field of play. From the moment an umpire or a referee enters the field of play they are bound by the field of play conduct and procedures.

任何在观众和媒体（记者、电视台和摄影师）视线下看得见和可能发生的都被视作是比赛区域的。裁判员和裁判长在到达比赛区域的那一刻应遵循下列临场准则和程序。

The actions and performance of every umpire on the field of play must be uniform in all aspects - not just in conducting a match but also on the way they walk to/from the assigned courts, performing their pre- and post- match duties as well as interactions with players, spectators and other officials on the field of play.

在临场，所有的裁判员的行为和表现必须统一，不仅在执裁时，而且在进 / 出指定的场地，履行赛前、赛后的职责以及在比赛区域与选手、观众和其他官员打交道时均应统一。

PRE-MATCH PREPARATIONS
裁判员赛前准备

Umpires should report to the Referee - or designated

assistant who handles umpire schedules - at least 30 minutes before the start of their assigned session, to prepare and getready for performing their duties.

裁判员应在自己被指派执法的那节比赛前 30 分钟向裁判长或指定的负责安排裁判任务的助理报到，做好执裁的准备。

The umpire is responsible for pre-match ball selection, racket inspection, as well as shirt (including advertisements), and in doubles/team, shorts or skirt check. He or she should also check the players' numbers if they are to be used. He or she should conduct these duties at the designated area at least 15 minutes before the start of a match.

裁判员负责比赛用球的挑选，检查球拍、服装（包括广告）、双打 / 团体比赛中短裤和短裙。还要检查运动员的号码布，如果要求佩戴的话。至少在赛前 15 分钟在指定的区域履行这些职责。

Approximately ten minutes before the start of each match the umpire should be ready with the scoresheet and balls for his or her designated table.

大约在赛前 10 分钟，裁判员应拿到指定球台的记分单和选好的比赛用球。

Before entering the field of play, the umpire and assis tant umpire should confer and discuss any issues pertaining to the upcoming match. They should agree on who will time the warm up period, intervals between games (typically the assistant umpire) and who will time the time-outs taken (typically the umpire). They should both be clear on how they will communicate during a match without necessarily having to confer physically between points or between games.

进入比赛区域前，裁判员与副裁判员应就任何与将要进行的比赛有关的问题进行讨论和交流，就谁控制练习时间、局间间歇时间（一般是副裁判员）和谁控制暂停时间（一般是裁判员）达成一致意见。双方应清楚如何在该场比赛中进行交流，而不必在回合间或局间非得借助语言或行动（等形式）。

Just before entering the field of play, the umpire and assistant umpire should line up near the field of play entrance and get set to walk in together as a team. The umpire should be in front with the scoresheet and ball box held in his or her left hand.

进入比赛区域前，裁判员和副裁判员应在赛区入口处排成一队准备一起入场，裁判员应站队伍前，左手拿着记分单和一盒球。

Neither the umpire nor the assistant umpire should be carrying anything else in their hands into the field of play. Everything an umpire and assistant umpire require to conduct their on-court duties - pen, stop watch, net gauges (plastic and weighted), yellow/red/white cards, coin, towel - should be in their pockets and not externally visible or dangling from the uniform or around the neck. Place all handbags and per sonal belongings in a designated area outside the field of play. The only exception to this may be rackets which have been tested and are carried in paper envelopes (or bags if envelopes are not available) by the umpire or assistant umpire. These should be carried as if they were a folder, not a bag.

进入比赛区域时，裁判员和副裁判员手里不能有其他任何东西，裁判器材，诸如笔、秒表、量网尺（塑料及金属）、黄/红/白牌、挑边器、毛巾应放在口袋内，不能露在外面或挂在制服或脖子上摇晃。将手提包和私人物品放到比赛区域外指定的地方。唯一的例外是，将已检测的球拍装入信封（没有信封时用袋子），由裁判员或副裁判员带入比赛区域。不应像袋子那样拎着，而应像文件夹那样携带。

When the umpire team is ready, they enter the field of play in a straight line, in uniform step, with the umpire leading the way to the assigned court. During the feature matches on the last day there may be appropriate introductory music announcing the presentation of the players and officials to the field of play.

当裁判队伍准备好时，裁判员带领整个队伍，迈着整齐的步伐，直线进入指定的赛区。在最后一天比赛的主要场次中，可能会有适当的引导音乐，并介绍出场的运动员和裁判员。

With or without introductory music, the umpire team should walk in a straight line, calmly, with deliberate step, and nominal hand motions. The objective is not to emulate a military parade, but rather a spirit that a unified team is on the way to perform an assigned task.

无论有无引导音乐，裁判员队伍均应迈着稳健的步伐、轻微地摆臂直线前进。这样做的目的不是模仿军队阅兵，而是为了体现一种精神，即一支统一的队伍正准备执行任务。

It is usual that there will be an assembly of a group of umpires to enter the field of play as a team - each proceeding to their respective table. In that case, umpires and assistant umpires will assemble at the designated staging area. Umpire teams will line up in order of their table assignments and walk into the field of play as a group, in step, following the first person in line.

通常各组裁判员会排成一队同时入场，再走向各自的球台。在这种情况下，裁判员和副裁判员在指定的区域集合。裁判员队伍应按照球台的顺序排好队，步调一致，一个接一个地进入比赛区域。

As each team of officials reaches their respective court they turn and go toward the umpire's chair. Upon entering the court, the umpires stand until all umpire teams have arrived at their respective positions.

当每组裁判员到达各自的区域，并走向裁判椅。一进入赛区，裁判员和副裁判员即应站立直到所有裁判员都到达指定的位置。

An umpire should never step over any barrier. He or she should always open a space between two barriers, step around gently, and close that space after passing through.

裁判员决不要跨越挡板，应该在两个挡板之间打开一个空隙，优雅地走过，而后关上这个空隙。

ARRIVING AT COURT

到达比赛场地

There may be a designated entry point for the umpire team to enter each court. Typically the entry point into each court should be one of the nearest corners on the side of the umpire's chair.

每块场地都会有指定的裁判队伍出入口。出入口一般是在每块场地靠近裁判椅最近的角落。

Upon entering the court, the umpire team walks toward the umpire's chair. The umpire stands on the furthest side of the umpire's chair, with scoresheet and balls in hand, feet together and hands to the side. The assistant umpire stands on the other side of the umpire's chair. This procedure is to be followed in the absence of any alternative directive by the referee. When available, the field of play announcer should present the umpires to the spectators and the media by name and association.

一进入赛区，裁判员和副裁判员都应该走向裁判椅。裁判员应站在裁判椅离入口较远的一侧，手拿记分单和球，以立正的姿势，将手放在身体两侧；副裁判员以同样的姿势站在裁判椅的另一侧。在裁判长没有其他要求时，按照以上流程和站位。如有条件，场地广播员应向观众和媒体介绍裁判员的姓名和协会。

As each name is called the official takes one small step forward and one step back to the same position. Do not turn around to face other spectators, bow, or make hand motions.

被叫到名字的裁判员向前迈一小步，再后退一小步回到原来的位置，不要向后转面对其他观众、鞠躬或举手示意。

Regardless whether the umpire team was or was not presented to the spectators, they should stand in that position for at least 5 seconds before starting their pre-match procedures. The assistant umpire should follow the lead of the umpire so that both can begin their on-court duties at the same time.

不管是否向观众介绍，入场的裁判员队伍应在到达指定位置、开始赛前程序前停留至少5秒钟，副裁判员应跟随前面的裁判员，这样他们可以同时开始执行临场的职责。

Under some conditions - typically during feature matches -players will also walk in with or after the umpire team. The normal order is umpire-players-assistant umpire. In that case, players, pairs or teams would stand next to the umpire and the other players, pairs or teams would stand next to the assistant umpire. After the players and umpires have been presented, pre-match procedures can begin.

在某些时候，特别是重要的比赛，运动员将与裁判员一起入场。通常的次序是：裁判员—运动员—副裁判员。在此情况下，一名/对/队运动员将站在裁判员的一侧，另一名/对/队运动员站在副裁判员的一侧。当介绍完运动员与裁判员后，再开始执行赛前职责。

PRE-MATCH PROCEDURE

赛前程序

Before the start of the warm up period, the umpire should:

Complete racket checks. If rackets have been checked pre-match, which will be the case in most major tournaments, rackets will be brought to the table in paper envelopes (or bags). Take the rackets out of the envelopes, and place the rackets on the same half of the table for the players to pick up. Do not hand the envelopes containing the rackets to the players. For full details of workflow procedures regarding racket checking please refer to the URC page of the ITTF web site.

Check shirt colour, if not completed during the ball selection

Check player numbers or names, if required by the Referee or organising committee

Confirm the designated advisor for non-team events

Perform the coin toss to determine serving/receiving and choice of ends

Ensure the assistant umpire is ready to start the stop-watch for the practice period if he or she is keep time

Complete the relevant information on the scoresheet

Sit in the umpire's chair for the duration of the practice period.

开始练习前，裁判员应该：

完成球拍检查。在大部分重要赛事中，球拍已于赛前检查并装入信封（纸袋）带到球台。从信封拿出两块球拍，放在球台同一侧台区，由运动员取回。不要将装有球拍的信封递给运动员。请查看国际乒联网站中国际乒联裁委会的网页，以了解详细工作流程；

如果在挑球时没有完成短袖运动衫颜色的检查，则继续完成；

检查运动员的号码或名字，如果裁判长或组委会要求佩戴；

单项比赛，确定场外指导者；

使用挑边器进行抽签，确定发球、接发球次序和方位；

如果副裁判员对练习时间进行计时，确保他（她）准备开表；

完成记分单上相关信息的填写；

选手练习时，裁判员坐在裁判椅上。

While the umpire is conducting his or her duties with the players, the assistant umpire should:

Ensure the point and game indicators are cleared to blank. Once both players or pairs are present in the court change the game indicators to 0-0

Check the net height and tension

Check the cleanliness of the table and floor - remove any debris

Organise and straighten out surrounds

Place name cards in proper place, if provided by the referee or organising committee

Start the stop-watch as soon as the practice starts

Sit in the assistant umpire's chair during the remainder of the practice period.

当裁判员在履行上述职责时，副裁判员应该：

确保比分和局分无显示。当双方运动员到达赛场时，将翻分器上的局分调至 0∶0；

检查网的高度和张力；

检查球台和地板是否干净，拿走任何碎屑；

将挡板摆放整齐；

如果裁判长或组委会提供了名牌，将它们放在合适的地方；

练习一开始，立即启动秒表；

完成上述职责后，在选手练习期间，副裁判员坐在副裁判员椅子上。

Occasionally the umpire's chair does not have a table or place to put the scoresheet. In this case it is recommended that the assistant umpire completes the scoresheet.

有时裁判员座椅上没有小台板或地方放置记分单，在这种情况下推荐副裁判员完成记分单的填写。

START OF THE MATCH

开始比赛

At the start of the first game:

When time is up, whoever is keeping the time should raise his or her hand and call "Time"

Ensure that the server has the ball before making any announcement. Do not ask for the ball back before making the announcement and then subsequently give it back after the announcement as this is not a good presentation.

When the server is ready, glance to see that the receiver is ready

Announce

"Keen versus Boll"

"First game"

Point to the server and call;

"Keen to serve"

"Love all" or "Zero-Zero"

第一局比赛开始：

当练习时间到，负责计时的裁判员或副裁判员举起手臂并宣布"时间到"。

在宣告前确保发球员已拿到球。不要在宣告前向运动员要回球，在宣告后又扔给他。因为这样不太好看。

当发球员准备好时，看一下接发球员是否准备好。

裁判员宣布：

“凯恩对波尔

“第 1 局比赛”

指向发球员并报：

“凯恩发球”

“0 比 0”。

The assistant umpire then changes the score to 0-0, starts the stop-watch, and the match begins.

副裁判员将比分调到 0∶0，启动秒表，比赛开始。

The umpire should make every effort to pronounce the name of each player correctly. If unsure about the pronunciation - ask the player while conducting racket check.

裁判员应尽量准确地报出每个运动员的名字。如果发音不确定，应在检查球拍时询问该运动员。

In a team match substitute the player's name with the team name.

在团体赛中用队名代替运动员姓名。

DURING MATCH PROCEDURE

比赛过程中

See diagram in Appendix E for proper and uniform hand signals, and explanation of when and how to use them.

正确和统一的手势以及何时、如何使用这些手势的解释参见附录 E 中的图表。

During the match, the umpire should:

Call the score in a clear and audible voice at a level that a person sitting at the coach's chair can hear and understand the calls

Time the play or designate the assistant umpire to time each game

Monitor and enforce the service laws

Monitor and enforce the behaviour regulations

Make sure the players leave the rackets on the table between games, unless it is strapped to their hand

Make sure play is continuous with no excessive delays during towelling or time out periods

Monitor and enforce the coaching laws. Between points and particularly during a change of service or ends, the umpire should turn his or her head and look at both coaches. Alternately, the umpire and assistant umpire can agree - before the match starts - that each one will monitor the coach that is best visible to them, or the one on their right

During authorised intervals the assistant umpire collects the ball and hands it to the umpire to retain until the end of the interval.

在比赛过程中，裁判员应做到：

报分清楚洪亮，坐到教练员席的人能听到并听懂报分。

控制比赛时间，或指定副裁判员来控制每局比赛时间。

监督并确保发球合法。

监督并确保选手的行为合法。

在局与局之间，确保选手的球拍放在球台上，除非球拍绑在运动员的手上。

确保比赛的连续性，擦汗、暂停的时间不能超出规定。

监督并确保教练员的指导合法。在分与分之间，特别是交换发球和方位时，裁判员应转过头去监督双方的指导者。或者，裁判员与副裁判员可在赛前达成一致，各自监督自己方便观察的指导者或在其右方的指导者。

在比赛许可的间歇时间，副裁判员捡回比赛用球，将其交给裁判员保管直至间歇时间结束。

END OF GAME PROCEDURE

一局比赛结束

At the end of a game the umpire should:

Call the score, point to winner, and announce “Game to Keen”

Record the score on the score card

The assistant umpire collects the ball and hands it to the umpire to retain until the start of the next game.

在一局比赛结束时，裁判员应该：

报出比分，指向获胜方，并宣布“该局凯恩获胜”

在记分单上记录比分。

副裁判员捡回比赛用球并递给裁判员，直至下局比赛开始。

START OF GAME PROCEDURE

一局比赛开始

At the start of other games the umpire should:

Hand the ball to the server

When the server is ready, glance to see that the receiver

is ready

Announce

“Second game”

Point to the server and call;

“Boll to serve”

“Love all” or “Zero-Zero”

The assistant umpire changes the score to 0-0, starts the stop-watch, and the game begins.

下一局比赛开始，裁判员应该：

将球扔给发球员。

当发球员准备好时，看一下接发球员是否准备好。

宣布“第 2 局比赛”。

指向发球员并报：“波尔发球”

“0 比 0”

副裁判员将比分调到 0∶0，启动秒表，比赛开始。

POST MATCH ANNOUNCEMEN

赛后宣布

At the end of a match the umpire should:

Call the score, point to winner, and announce “Game and match to Keen”

“Keen wins 4 games to 3”

and in a team match

“Netherlands leads by 1 match to 0” or “Netherlands and Germany 1 match all”

一场比赛结束，裁判员应：

报完比分，指向获胜方，并宣布“凯恩胜该局和该场比赛”

“凯恩以 4∶3 胜该场比赛”

在团体比赛

“荷兰队以 1∶0 领先”或“荷兰和德国 1∶1 平”。

POST MATCH PROCEDURE

赛后操作程序

After the match the umpire should:

Record the score on the scoresheet

Obtain the players’ signatures in an individual match or the team captains’ signatures in a team match (if required by referee)

The assistant umpire returns the score indicator to blank, collects the balls, racket(s) if necessary and returns the court to a proper condition.

比赛结束，裁判员应该：

在记分单上记录比分。

单项比赛裁判员应要求运动员在记分单上签名，团体比赛需要队长的签名（如果裁判长要求）。

副裁判员将比分显示器回复为空白。收好比赛用球和球拍（如果需要），将场地条件恢复到合适的状况。

END OF MATCH - UMPIRES WALKING OUT

比赛结束——裁判员退场

The umpire and assistant umpire meet at the umpire’s chair or table and stand so that the umpire leads the way out without having to cross the path of the assistant umpire.

裁判员和副裁判员在裁判椅或桌处集合，裁判员靠近出口一侧，由他（她）带领副裁判员离开，而无须穿越副裁判的线路。

The umpire leads the way with the scoresheet in the left hand and the assistant umpire following in step with the umpire - no accompanied music.

裁判员左手拿记分单在前，副裁判员随后，退场时没有音乐伴随。

The umpire team returns the scoresheet correctly completed directly to the referee's desk for signature. The referee (or designated deputy referee on duty) should check the scoresheet for completeness and accuracy; sign the card and forward it for results processing.

裁判员和副裁判员将填写正确的记分单直接交裁判长席签字。裁判长（或指定的值班副裁判长）应检查记分单是否填写完整和正确；签字后送成绩处理处。

Umpires should not linger or walk around the field of play once their assigned duties are completed. If they wish to watch other matches in progress, they should proceed outside the field of play to the viewing areas open for officials and spectators.

裁判员在结束执裁任务后不应该在赛场内逗留或闲逛，如果他们希望观看其他正在进行的比赛，应该退出赛区到为官员和观众开放的观看区域去。

SUMMARY

小结

While on the field of play - for any reason - umpires,

referees and evaluators should be in designated dress code or uniforms, alert and aware of their surroundings, and mindful how their presence and conversations might affect ongoing play or visual perceptions.

不管任何理由，凡出现在比赛区域的裁判员、裁判长、评估师必须穿着指定服装或制服，时刻警觉周围环境，留意由于他们的出现及交谈给比赛的进行和视觉所带来的影响。

Umpires should refrain from engaging players in idle chat before, during or after a match. An umpire may respond to a player's question or explain a call made but should not initiate a discussion on non-match related matters.

裁判员应避免在赛前、赛中或赛后和运动员闲聊。裁判员应回答运动员的疑问，或解释判分的依据，但决不允许挑起与比赛无关的话题。

While in uniform, officials should be mindful that they represent their associations and, most importantly, that their actions reflect on all officials. During international events, all foreign umpires are guests of the host association and should respect their traditions and social customs inside and outside the field of play.

当比赛官员身穿统一制服时，应注意他们自己所代表的协会，更重要的是他们的行为将会给所有官员带来影响。在国际赛事中，所有来访裁判员都是主办方的客人，无论赛场内外，他们都应当尊重当地的传统和风俗习惯。

Under no circumstances should umpires engage spectators or members of the media with matters relating to their conduct or the conduct of other officials. All such matters should be directed to the referee or Tournament Director.

在任何情况下，裁判员都不能因自己或其他竞赛官员的行为与观众或媒体工作人员直接发生关联。遇到类似的情况应直接报告裁判长或竞赛主任。

Appendix G——Uniform for International Umpires

附录 G——国际级裁判员的制服

The ITTF Umpires and Referees Committee (URC) has adopted the following uniform colour combinations for umpires working ITTF World Title events.

对于执法国际乒联世界级赛事的裁判员，国际乒联裁委会采用了下列制服颜色组合。

International Umpires working ITTF non-world title events may wear their National Uniform (if one exists) or the ITTF International Umpire Uniform.

执法国际乒联非世界级赛事的国际级裁判员可以穿着自己国家协会的制服（如果有的话）或国际乒联国际级裁判员的制服。

It is the responsibility of each International Umpire - or their National Association - to provide the recommended uniform in order for them to represent their association at World Title Events.

每位国际级裁判员或其所属协会有责任配备好推荐的制服以代表所属协会参加世界级的比赛。

The objective of a uniform dress code for ITTF International Umpires across multiple associations is not to stifle individuality, self-expression or national identity, but to have near uniformity in presentation of officials for spectators and TV coverage.

为国际乒联下属众多协会的国际级裁判员制定着装标准的目的不是抑制个性、自我表现或国家特征，而是把比赛官员近乎一致地展示给观众和电视转播。

Standard full dress Umpire uniform for working in mild / air-conditioned environments

	Men	Women
Jacket / Blazer	Solid Navy Blue single breasted - tailored jacket / blazer	
Shirt / Blouse	Light blue dress shirt with collar	Light blue dress blouse with collar
Pants / Skirt	Khaki / Tan dress pants / trousers ***	Khaki / Tan dress skirt or pants
Tie	Red Tie - with optional ITTF logo	Red scarf or tie - with optional ITTF logo
Belt - if worn	Black dress / leather belt with a small buckle	
Shoes	Black dress or sports shoes with non-marking soles. High heeled shoes are not to be worn.	
Socks	Black ankle length or higher socks	Hosiery when worn with skirt
Sweater (Optional for cold weather)	Solid Navy Blue sweater worn under the jacket if the temperature inside or outside the playing hall is too cold.	
Badge / Pin	The ITTF International Umpire Badge / Pin - worn on the left lapel of the jacket.	
Other badge / pin (optional)	Only one other badge / pin that is smaller in size than the IU badge / pin representing the home association. Worn on the right lapel. There should be no other patches identifying home Associations, region, and membership in other organizations or participation in previous events.	

(continued table)

	Men	Women
Other National and International credentials	While working as an International Umpire, only the IU badge / pin should be worn even if the umpire has other national or international qualifications (i.e. National or International Referee)	
Hats and other head gear	None - unless approved by the Referee	
Name tag	A white nametag with black lettering in Times New Roman font with the last name all in CAPITAL / UPPERCASE letters, followed by a comma then the first name (or preferred name) in lower case letters with the first letter capitalized. The nametag should be 2 cm wide by 8 cm long and is worn on the right lapel of the jacket about the same height as the IU badge / pin.	
Examples of name tags One LAST name and one first name	DILLON, Steven	
Two first names	MOHAMMED, Hassan-Ibrahim	
Two LAST names and two first names	LIEBANA ANDRES, Juan-Carlos	
One first name & nickname (in brackets)	ZHANG, Cheong (Joe)	
Two first names with a nickname	ZAKI, Mohammed Hassan (MO)	
Junior, Senior, III	ZIPPER, José (Jr.)	
Compound LAST name	LAI-FATT, Liu	
Compound LAST name and two first names	ABDEL-MEGEED, Khaled-Ali	

***O'Reilly colour codes (http://www.oreilly.com/catalog/wdnut/excerpt/color_names.html) for Khaki and Tan is used as reference. These are the colours used by programmers to define colours for computer screens.

The RGB / HEX values (http://www.colorschemer.com/on-line.html) are also included as a reference.

tan
RGB Value – 210,180,140 HEX Value – D2B48C

khaki
RGB Value – 240,230,140 HEX Value – F0E68C

在气候温和 / 有空调的工作环境下的标准裁判服正装

	男	女
夹克 / 西装上衣	单排扣**深蓝色**夹克 / 西装上衣	
衬衫 / 女式衬衫	**浅蓝色**有领西装衬衫	**浅蓝色**有领女式西装衬衫
裤子 / 裙子	**土黄色 / 褐色**西装裤 ***	**土黄色 / 褐色**西装裙 / 裤
领带	红色领带——可选择有国际乒联标志的	红色丝巾——可选择有国际乒联标志的
腰带——如果佩戴	**黑色**小搭扣西装 / 皮腰带	
鞋子	**黑色**鞋底不留痕的皮鞋或运动鞋，不能穿高跟鞋	
袜子	**黑色**脚踝高度或更高些的袜子	穿裙子时的裤袜
毛衣（天冷时选择）	如果比赛大厅内外的温度很低时，穿在夹克衫里面的深蓝色毛衣	

（续表）

	男	女
徽章 / 别针	国际乒联国际级裁判员徽章 / 别针——别在夹克衫的左领上	
其他徽章 / 别针（可选择）	只能有 1 个代表所属协会的徽章和别针，尺寸小于国际级裁判员徽章 / 别针，别在右领上。不能有所属协会、地区、其他组织的会员或参加先前赛事的其他表示	
其他国家和国际资历	工作职责是裁判员时，只能佩戴国际级的徽章 / 别针，即使该裁判员还有其他国家级或国际级的资历（例如国家级裁判长或国际级裁判长）	
帽子和其他头饰	无——除非得到裁判长的许可	
姓名牌	白底黑字，新罗马字体，姓氏所有字母大写，后跟逗号，名字第一个字母大写，其余字母小写 姓名牌 2 厘米宽，8 厘米长，别在夹克衫的右领上，与国际级徽章 / 别针同高	
姓名牌的例子		
1 个姓和 1 个名	DILLON, Steven	
2 个名字	MOHAMMED, Hassan-Ibrahim	
2 个姓和 2 个名	LIEBANA ANDRES, Juan-Carlos	
1 个名和昵称 (括弧内)	ZHANG, Cheong (Joe)	
2 个名和昵称	ZAKI, Mohammed Hassan (MO)	
一世，二世，三世	ZIPPER, José (Jr.)	
复合姓	LAI-FATT, Liu	
复合姓和 2 个名	ABDEL-MEGEED, Khaled-Ali	

*** 土黄色和褐色采用 O'Reilly（http://www.oreilly.com/catalog/wdnut/excerpt/color_names.html）颜色标准作为参考。编程员用这些颜色来界定计算机屏幕的色彩。

三原色和 16 进制值（http://www.colorschemer.com/online.html）也被用作参考。

Standard light dress Umpire uniform for working in hot / non air conditioned environments

	Men	Women
Jacket / Blazer	None	
Shirt / Blouse	Light blue short-sleeve dress shirt with collar. NO T-SHIRTS.	Light blue dress blouse with collar
Pants / Skirt	Khaki / Tan dress pants / trousers	Khaki / Tan dress skirt or pants
Tie	None	
Belt - if worm	Black dress / leather belt with a small buckle	
Shoes	Black dress or sports shoes with non-marking soles.	
Socks	Black ankle length socks	Hosiery when worn with skirt
Badge / Pin	The ITTF International Umpire Badge / Pin - worn on the left side of the shirt.	
Other badge / pin (optional)	Only one other badge / pin that is smaller in size than the IU badge / pin representing the home association. Worn just below the name tag	
Name tag	A white nametag with black lettering (same as above) worn on the right side of the dress shirt at about the same height as the IU pin.	

在气候炎热 / 无空调的工作环境下的标准夏季裁判服

	男	女
夹克 / 西装上衣	无	
衬衫 / 女式衬衫	浅蓝色有领短袖衬衫。T 恤衫不可以	浅蓝色有领短袖女式衬衫
裤子 / 裙子	土黄色 / 褐色西装裤	土黄色 / 褐色西装裙 / 裤
领带	无	
腰带——如果佩戴	黑色小搭扣西装 / 皮腰带	
鞋子	黑色鞋底不留痕的皮鞋或运动鞋	
袜子	黑色脚踝高度的袜子	穿裙子时的裤袜
徽章 / 别针	国际乒联国际级裁判员徽章 / 别针——别在夹克衫的左领上	
其他徽章 / 别针（可选择）	只能有 1 个代表所属协会的徽章和别针，尺寸小于国际级裁判员徽章 / 别针。别在姓名牌下	
姓名牌	白底黑字（同上），别在西装衬衫的右边，与国际级裁判员徽章同高	

Appendix H——Para Table Tennis Rules and Regulations

附录 H——残疾人乒乓球规则和规程

This Appendix has been added in view of the merger of IPTTC with ITTF. The laws and regulations are now an integral part of the ITTF rules. For further information on ITTF Para Table Tennis Division please go to the ITTF website http://www.ittf.com Main Page and click on the Para TT tab.

鉴于国际残疾人乒乓球委员会与国际乒联合并，增加了附录 H，其规则和规程现在是国际乒联规则必不可少的一部分。了解更多有关国际残疾人乒乓球部的信息请查阅国际乒联网站 http://www.ittf.com 主页，点击 Para TT tab.

GENERAL

Athletes with a disability are separated into classes, depending on lesions and limitations described in a classification system. An international classification panel is responsible for classifying players at international events.

- Class 1—5 for wheelchair players
- Class 6—10 for standing players
- Class 11 for players with an intellectual disability

The lower the number of the class, the more severe the disability.

通常

根据分级系统描述的器官损伤和身体活动限制，残疾运动员被分成不同的等级。国际分级小组负责在国际比赛中对运动员进行分级。

- 1—5 级是轮椅组运动员。
- 6—10 级是站立组运动员。
- 11 级是智障运动员。

等级越低，残疾程度越严重。

After they have been classified at an international level, all players hold an international classification card (ICC) that specifies the sport class and sport class status. The ICC contains sections indicating any physical limitations (e.g. in making a legal service) or permanent requirements for medical reasons (strapping, binding, corset, modified wheelchair).

在国际比赛被分级后，所有运动员都有自己的国际分级卡（ICC）注明运动等级和运动等级状况。国际分级卡上还有专门区域指明任何生理限制（如在合法发球方面）或由于医疗原因的永久需求（捆、绑、紧身衣，改造的轮椅）。

If a player plays in an international championship for the first time and does not have an ICC, his or her Association will give him or her a temporary classification. He or she will be then classified at the championships and be assigned a sports class and sports class status. It is also sometimes necessary for players, over time, to be reclassified due to a progressive disability or lesser disability due to recovery. They are specified in a list communicated to the appointed Classifiers, Referee and Organising Committee before the relevant tournament. The classification or review for specified players is organised by classifiers the day before the start of the tour nament and is concluded before the referee conducts the draw for the singles events, taking into account any changes to players' classification.

如果运动员第一次参加国际锦标赛时没有国际分级卡，他（她）的协会将提供一张临时分级卡，然后在该锦标赛中被分级，赋予运动等级和运动等级状态。由于伤残的逐渐发展或康复，一段时期后，运动员有时也需要被重新分级。在相关比赛开始前，会在通知指定分级师、裁判长和组委会的名单中具体说明。比赛前一天分级师会安排相关运动员的分级和审查，并在裁判长单项抽签之前完成，以便将运动员分级的任何变化考虑进去。

If a player has deliberately misled the classifiers he or she may not be permitted to compete at the discretion of the Referee and may face further sanctions from the ITTF.

如果运动员有意误导分级师，他（她）有可能被裁判长不允许参加比赛，并可能面临国际乒联进一步的惩罚。

WHEELCHAIRS

轮椅

Wheelchairs must have at least two large wheels and one small wheel at the start of a rally. If, for any reason during a match, any wheels on the player's wheelchair become dislodged and the wheelchair has no more than two wheels, then the rally must be stopped immediately and a point awarded to his or her opponent.

在一个回合开始前，轮椅必须有至少两个大轮和一个小轮。如果赛中出于任何原因，运动员轮椅上的轮子移动，轮椅只剩两个轮子，则该回合必须被中止，并判对方得 1 分。

In individual and team events, no part of the body above the knees may be attached to the chair as this could improve balance. However, should a player require some strapping or binding for medical reasons, this must be noted on his or her classification card and it will be taken into account when assessing the player's sports class.

在单项和团体赛中，膝盖以上身体的任何部位都不能绑在轮椅上，因为这会增加平衡。然而运动员出于医疗原因需要某些捆绑时，必须在他（她）的分级卡中指明，并在对运动员进行运动等级评估时加以考虑。

The height of one or maximum two cushions is limited to 15cm in playing conditions with no other addition to the wheelchair.

比赛时，轮椅上有 1 个或最多 2 个坐垫，高度限制在 15 厘米以内，不能有其他附加物。

If a player must use a belt (around the waist) and/or a corset due to his or her disability, he or she must prove that it is required to the satisfaction of the classification panel. The onus is on the player to draw attention to the use of such equipment to the Chief Classifier either for the initial or review of classification. Permission for use of a belt and / or a corset may be given under the following conditions:

如果运动员由于伤残必须使用腰带或紧身衣，他（她）必须提出相关证据并得到分级小组的满意。运动员有责任在首次分级或分级审核时让首席分级师注意使用这些装备。以下条件可以允许使用腰带或紧身衣：

• permanent - this must be written on the player's international classification card (ICC) by the Chief Classifier at the relevant international tournament.

• 永久——在相关比赛中必须由首席分级师注明在运动员的国际分级卡上。

• temporary - the player must provide a full explanation from his or her own doctor who must certify the period which the belt and/or corset is/are required. This certificate must be signed and dated by the medical doctor and submitted to the Chief Classifier at the relevant tournament. The player must report this to the Referee before the start of competition in which he or she participates.

• 临时——动员必须提供他（她）的医生的证明，详细解释该运动员在一段时期内需要佩戴腰带和/或紧身衣。这个证明必须由医生签字和注明日期，然后提交给相关比赛的首席分级师。运动员必须在其参加的比赛开始前将证明报告给裁判长。

Should additions of supporting structures be made to the wheelchair, whether attached to the wheelchair or not (except cushions), players must ask for a classification or a re-classification in this modified wheelchair. Any additions to the wheelchair without re-classification and authorization written on the ICC shall be considered as illegal and the player may be disqualified.

如果在轮椅上添加额外的支撑结构物，无论是否固定在轮椅上（坐垫除外），运动员必须为这辆改装的轮椅要求分级或重新分级。任何对轮椅的增添如果没有重新分级并在国际分级卡上注明得到许可，将被认为是非法并且运动员可能被取消资格。

Tables shall allow access to wheelchairs without obstructing the player's legs and shall allow access to two wheelchairs for doubles.

乒乓球台应允许轮椅进入且不妨碍运动员的双脚，双打比赛时球台能允许两辆轮椅进入。

PRE-MATCH PREPARATION

赛前准备

For matches involving players in a wheelchair, the umpire should also check:

轮椅运动员的比赛，裁判员应检查：

- The number of wheels on the wheelchair
- 轮椅轮子的数量。
- The player does not have his or her backpack on the back of the wheelchair
- 轮椅背后不能有运动员背包。
- The height of the player's cushion or 2 cushions
- 座垫或两个座垫的高度。
- The player is wearing tracksuit pants and no jeans
- 运动员着运动裤（非牛仔裤）。
- The player has his or her name and 3 letter code for the association on the back of his or her shirt
- 运动衫背面有运动员名字和协会的缩写（3 个字母）。

LAWS FOR STANDING PLAY

站立组比赛规则

There are no exceptions to the laws of table tennis for standing players with a disability. All players play according to the laws and regulations of the ITTF. On the classification cards there is a section indicating what limitations, if any, a player has in making a legal serve.

乒乓球规则对站立组残疾运动员没有例外。所有运动员按照国际乒联的规则和规程进行比赛。分级卡上有专门区域指出运动员受限制的缘由，如果没有的话，运动员发球将适用合法发球规则。

MATCH CONDUCT

For a player, adequate medical recovery time, but in no circumstances more than 10 minutes, may be allowed by the Referee after consulting the Classifier or medical doctor at the tournament, if the player is unable to play temporarily due to the nature of his or her disability or condition.

比赛管理

如果运动员因残疾或身体条件的性质而暂时丧失比赛能力，裁判长在征询医学分级师或赛会医生的意见后，可以允许足够的医疗恢复时间，但无论如何不能超过 10 分钟。

Appendix I——A Summary of Law and Regulation Changes since 2011

附录 I——自 2011 年以来规则和规程变化摘要

The main changes made to laws and regulations since 2011 are:

自 2011 年以来规则和规程的主要变化

LAWS

规则

The net must be attached to the supporting posts from top to bottom.

球网两端必须整体与网柱完全相连。

In doubles if only one of the pair is in a wheelchair then, after the return of service, either player of that pair can make returns. However no part of the player's wheelchair, nor the foot of the standing player, can cross the centre line of the table or it is a point to their opponent.

在双打中，当配对中至少有一名运动员由于残疾而坐轮椅时，发球员应先发球，接发球员应还击，此后该配对的任何一名运动员均可还击。然而，该配对中，运动员轮椅及站立运动员脚部的任何部分均不能超越球台中线的假定延长线。如果超越，裁判员将判对方得 1 分。

REGULATIONS

规程

Racket control centre and racket testing have been modified and are now the responsibility of the URC.

球拍检测中心和球拍检测的条款已修改，球拍检测现在是国际乒联裁委会的职责。

Advertisements and Markings within the playing area have been modified.

比赛区域广告和标记物的条款已修改。